CENTRAL CITY AND GILPIN COUNTY

Then and Now

CENTRAL CITY AND GILPIN COUNTY

Then and Now

by

Robert L. Brown

Cover Design by Teresa Sales

The CAXTON PRINTERS, Ltd.
Caldwell, Idaho
1994

Brown, Robert L., 1921–
    Central City and Gilpin County : then and now / by Robert L.
Brown.
        p.   cm.
    Includes bibliographical references (p.) and index.
    ISBN 0-87004-363-3
    1. Central City (Colo.)--History. 2. Central City (Colo.)--
History--Pictorial works. 3. Gilpin County (Colo.)--History.
4. Gilpin County (Colo.)--History--Pictorial works. 5. Gilpin
County (Colo.)--Gold discoveries.   I. Title.
    F784.C4B76   1994   94-15643
    978.8'62--dc20   CIP

Lithographed and bound in the United States of America by
The CAXTON PRINTERS, Ltd.
Caldwell, ID 83605-3299
158432

For my sister, Vivian Brown Vetra, who loves and remembers all sorts of history.

CONTENTS

LIST OF ILLUSTRATIONS

PREFACE

THROUGHOUT HISTORY, gold has possessed a magic of its own. Although several discoveries of gold were made in America previous to 1859, notably in Georgia, California, and Nevada, any rumor that someone had found the yellow metal in a new place was sufficient to start a migration of people, usually westward. The recent Panic of 1857 had left large numbers of impoverished Americans in its wake, people only too anxious for a fresh start somewhere else. So it was with those who came to Cherry Creek in western Kansas' Arapahoe County.

Prior to the Pikes Peak Gold Rush, such well-known persons as William Gilpin and Zebulon Pike, plus a few lesser-known souls, like the trapper, James Purcell, had reported minor gold finds within the western part of Kansas Territory's mountains.

Notable among those who listened to the enticing rumors were two vastly different men, William Greenberry Russell and John H. Gregory. Both men were Georgians, both were also veterans of the gold excitement in that state, who had chosen to try it once more in the rush to California. In the Golden State, Russell failed to find gold, although one account insists that he made enough to pay for his brother's medical education. Gregory, on the other hand, did fairly well near Sutter's Mill.

Persistent accounts describing the easy riches to be found near Cherry Creek in the 1850s sent gold-hungry farmers westward from Missouri and eastern Kansas. Among them were William Larimer of Leavenworth who stayed to bestow the Denver name on an infant settlement and to lay out its first streets. Colonel Ed Wynkoop led a party of men from Lecompton, Kansas, following Larimer's group. John Easter was a butcher from Lawrence, Kansas who heard stories of gold from a Delaware Indian visiting his shop. These were the men who led the first gold hunters to Cherry Creek.

In order to reach their destination, they and others followed the westbound wagon trails that already existed. Both the well-known Oregon and Santa Fe Trails had been utilized extensively by California–bound argonauts. To a lesser extent, the Mormon Trail, north of the Oregon road, was also used. The Santa Fe Trail was too far south to have been a practical choice, although some "Pikes Peakers," including Russell's party, followed it any-way. Similarly, the well-developed Oregon Trail crossed Wyoming, a like distance to the north. It was used extensively, as was the Platte River Road, which left the Oregon Trail and followed the river down into Denver City.

Shortest and most dangerous of all of the routes to Denver City was the Smoky Hill Trail, and old Indian hunting path that came almost straight west out of Kansas. Because it was shorter, it was destined to become a freighting and stagecoach road, as well as a scene of tragedy for some who chose to follow it.

This, then, was the setting: the background for the well-known Pikes Peak Gold Rush. Before it was over, a new territory called Colorado had evolved. It became a state in 1876. An impressive number of cities and towns grew up around the first Cherry Creek camps, which eventually coalesced to become Denver.

West of Denver there were enormously rich deposits of gold. The resulting influx of miners formed the beginnings of Central City and its surroundings: the so-called Richest Square Mile on Earth. Soon, Gilpin County evolved, with a population that sometimes approached 40,000 and Central City became the second largest community in Colorado. This book tells the story of this remarkable area, its towns, its mines, and its people.

ACKNOWLEDGEMENTS

INEVITABLY, THE WRITING OF ANY BOOK causes the author to incur many debts. First of all, special thanks must go to my wife of forty-nine years, Evelyn McCall Brown. She has been my companion on field trips, a source of advice on sentence structure, photographic angles, and has been of great help with proofreading. For the eleventh time, Freda and Francis Rizzari have given most generously of their time, skills, and knowledge of history by proofreading the final manuscript. As always, their competence and suggestions have been invaluable to me.

Many of the early photographs have come from the Rizzaris' collection. Others came from Frances and Dick Ronzio and from the late Fred and Jo Mazzulla. Nancy and Ed Bathke, Sid Squibb, Leo and Mitzi Stambaugh, and the Gilpin County Historical Society have also made photographs available to me. Likewise, the extensive photographic collections at the Western History Department of the Denver Public Library and the Library of the Colorado State Historical Society supplied pictures unobtainable elsewhere.

A majority of my research was done at the two previously named institutions. Books and other sources consulted are listed in the bibliography. The late Louis Carter of Central City was an invaluable source of information, as was the late Scott Whitman, a native of Nevadaville. Dorothy and Tom Lehre of Denver and Nevadaville gave me access to their research. Jack L. Morison has been a cheerful companion on several field trips around Gilpin County, as have been Barbara and Earl Boland. Others who have contributed to this book include Jane Bass, the late Mae Bertagnoli, the late Guy Herstrom, Jim Cozens, Dwight DeWitt, and Dr. and Mrs. William H. Anderson, Jr.

To all of these good friends and institutions, my sincere gratitude.

R.L.B.

CENTRAL CITY AND GILPIN COUNTY

Then and Now

1.

THE EARLIEST ARGONAUTS AND MOUNTAIN MEN

BY THE TIME GOLD WAS FOUND in Colorado's Gilpin County, the Rockies had been crossed and recrossed by treasure seekers for nearly three centuries. Actually, there was as yet no Colorado. Denver was a part of Kansas Territory, Breckenridge was in Utah, Boulder was within Nebraska, while most of southern Colorado belonged to New Mexico. Colorado Territory was not created by Congress until February of 1861.

The lure of easy riches has long been a powerful motive, one that has moved people to abandon farming, city life, or most any other calling to tempt Lady Luck in a prosaic search for gold. A Spaniard, Juan Rivera, was certainly one of the first to seek an El Dorado within what is now Colorado. The year was 1765, when Rivera traversed the San Juan Range and found a small quantity of precious metal. Researchers are still unsure about what it was that he located. Perhaps it was silver; possibly gold. Both these elements still exist in the San Juans. Although many in New Spain saw Rivera's samples, he was never able to find the source again. As the years passed, the Rivera find became just one among the multiplicity of San Juan "lost mine" stories.

Down in Santa Fe, in 1807, a fur trapper named James Purcell showed Lieutenant Zebulon Pike some gold nuggets he had picked up somewhere in South Park, probably along one of the branches of the South Platte River. The West's trappers and mountain men were a strange, independent, self-sufficient lot, with strict, narrow, hidebound ideas about anyone other than trappers. If a person was a real man he'd be a mountain man. Any who dug up the earth, be they farmer or miner, were less than nothing in their opinion. To register his contempt, Purcell carelessly threw the nuggets away. Pike both observed and recorded the incident in his journal.

Between 1842 and 1845, the explorer John Charles Fremont crossed present Colorado five times. Although he sought no gold himself, one member of his party, William Gilpin, probably met and spoke with trappers. For many years after his western travels, Gilpin told and retold the tales he had heard about gold in the high Rockies. Quite incidentally, at that time the Rockies were known as the Mexican Mountains. Curiously, these events aroused no particular interest when the Pike and Gilpin journals were published in the years after the War of 1812, our second war with Great Britain. Neither the Rivera nor the Purcell finds involved large quantities of precious metals. Besides, our post-war national economy would not justify sending expeditions out into an almost unknown wilderness to search for some rumored golden will-o'-the-wisp.

Although President Thomas Jefferson had wisely doubled our nation's size through the purchase of the disputed Louisiana Territory in 1803, much of this vast land was still unexplored. Jefferson dispatched his secretary, Meriwether Lewis, and the frontiersman William Clark westward in 1804–1806 to see what we had acquired. But this notable expedition explored only the northern portion of Louisiana, from St. Louis through to the Pacific Northwest. Lieutenant Pike was supposed to explore the southern part of Louisiana, but he may have been lost when he mistook the Red River for the Arkansas. In any case, he was captured by the Spanish and taken to Santa Fe, where he met James Purcell. Consequently, the land south of the forty-fifth parallel remained known only to a handful of explorers and mountain men.

America's first gold discovery of substance was one that would have a marked effect on the future Colorado. It was a big one, and thoroughly documented as well, but it wasn't even in the West. In 1827, would-be argonauts made their way south along the Atlantic seaboard, in order to be in on the ground floor of a significant gold discovery. It was in Dahlonega County, along the face of the Appalachian mountain chain in Georgia. In order to house the sudden influx of humanity, a town called Auraria came into being. There was just one overriding problem: the gold was on Cherokee Indian land. Therefore, as in later rushes, the Native Americans had to go. Most of them were placed on a reservation in present-day Oklahoma, then called Indian Territory. Georgia's gold country quickly opened up for exploitation.

Prominent among the dispossessed was William Greenberry Russell, a half-Cherokee who had worked for a time in the mines of Dahlonega County. His contemporaries referred to Russell as a squaw man, because his wife was a full-blooded member of the Cherokee Nation. Quite understandably, the Cherokees were embittered by their en masse removal from their ancestral homeland, in distinct violation of

Courtesy State Historical Society of Colorado Library

An unknown photographer took this likeness of William Green
Russell.

from their ancestral homeland, in distinct violation of a treaty signed earlier with official Washington.

When the word of James Marshall's accidental discovery of gold at John Augustus Sutter's saw mill filtered back from California in 1848–1849, Green Russell was more than a little interested. This was a far larger find than the one in Georgia. Russell was now a professional prospector with experience in mining. In California he saw a chance to redeem his own fortunes and perhaps help the Cherokee people, as well. He reasoned that his prior mining knowledge qualified him to make a big strike along the mother lode. Having done so, he hoped to return home with enough money to "hire a Philadelphia red-mouthed lawyer" to sue the government and get the Cherokee homeland returned to its rightful owners.

Green Russell and his two brothers, Levi and Oliver, started for California by way of the well-known Santa Fe Trail. Although they tried for nine years, they found no gold. Unfortunately, the Russell brothers were among the unlucky ones, the approximately ninety percent who regularly return empty-handed from any mining frontier. They did make a little money in the Golden State by working for others, enough to pay for their return to the East. But their efforts to reopen the Auraria mines exhausted their meager resources. Then came the Panic of 1857, and the Russells, with many other Americans, were impoverished.

Another Georgian, Lewis Ralston, decided to try his luck in California. In common with the Russells' experiences, he too was unable to locate a golden fortune. But Ralston recalled that on the way out to California he had found placer gold on what became Ralston Creek, which flows through present Arvada. The date was June 22, 1850. Upon returning to

Oklahoma a Cherokee preacher named John Beck, who had been with Ralston, began writing letters to relatives and friends in Georgia, urging formation of two parties to prospect around Ralston Creek. They met on the Arkansas River in June of 1858. Preacher Beck insisted that there should be no travel on the Sabbath. Fifty men from Oklahoma and twenty from Georgia made up the party. The three Russell brothers traveled with the Georgia group.

On Ralston Creek, the best they could do was about twenty-five cents per man each day. Prospecting on several other streams brought only discouragement. They also investigated the future site of Denver. Most of the Cherokees and some Anglos left for home on July 4. Thirty or more people left on July 7. Green Russell and twelve others decided to continue prospecting. They found a better placer gold deposit southeast of present-day Aurora. They established a small camp there and named it Russellville. The name persisted, and some mining continued there until 1930. Today, Russellville Gulch is full of condominiums.

Later, when rumors of a nearby Cheyenne war party reached them, the Russell party decided to split up to avoid a conflict. At that point they had been working for twenty–some days without resting, and many among them were disappointed. Besides, autumn was approaching and the days were becoming chilly. Some of them decided to return to the East. Green Russell and the rest continued the quest. On Little Dry Creek, in present-day Englewood, they made a modest placer gold find in a pocket where the creek empties into the South Platte River.

Meanwhile, a second party arrived in eleven prairie schooners. John Easter, a butcher from Lawrence, Kansas led the group. They established their camp on Dry Creek at its junction with the South Platte River. In his meat market one day, Easter overheard rumors being spread by Fall Leaf, a Delaware Indian, about gold being present where Cherry Creek empties into the South Platte. Easter pursued the subject with Fall Leaf, closed his shop and organized a party of eager would-be gold seekers.

Upon arrival, they met the Russell group. Prior to this get-together, neither party was aware of the others' presence. Although Russell assured Easter's people that the Dry Creek placer had been exhausted, the Lawrence group nevertheless decided to settle in for the winter at the Dry Creek site. Meanwhile, the Russells left for Wyoming. Easter's people erected cabins and named their settlement Montana City. It was the first town to take root on the future site of Denver. Its life span was a short one.

Within a relatively short time, a third party of Kansans appeared on the scene. General William Larimer led the group from Leavenworth when word arrived that there was gold in the western part of the territory. Larimer's group was much smaller than the Russell or the Easter parties, consisting of just six men in a single wagon. Their way west followed the northern branch of the Santa Fe Trail. Another group of gold seekers from Oskaloosa, Kansas joined them along the way. Near the deteriorating walls of Bents Fort they encountered another group, consisting of eleven men from Lecompton, Kansas, under the leadership of Colonel Ed Wynkoop. As expected, they also chose to follow the Larimer Party. On November 16, 1858, they arrived on Cherry Creek and settled in for the winter.

As the weather grew cooler, the Lawrence Party decided to abandon Montana City in favor of a town site at the mouth of Cherry Creek. They established

Saint Charles town site and began selling lots. At this point, their settlement was little more than a town on paper, an optimistic dream. Directly across Cherry Creek stood a second nucleus community known as Auraria, named in honor of the gold town back home in Georgia. To encourage its growth, Auraria offered building lots at no cost. A siege of cold weather caused most of the Lawrence party to abandon Saint Charles in favor of a warmer winter in Kansas. They left behind just one man, whose job it was to sell building lots in Saint Charles.

When Larimer appeared in mid–November he initially settled his people in Auraria. One dark night, Larimer crossed the creek to examine the Saint Charles site firsthand. He liked what he saw. Reasoning that it had been abandoned, Larimer decided to acquire it. The General got the hapless lot seller drunk on whiskey and promises, plus a few direct threats. Most reliable sources now agree that Larimer jumped the claim of the Saint Charles Town Company and took over. On April 5, 1860, the rival communities quit competing and initiated a moonlight ceremony on the Larimer Street bridge, uniting the two towns. Saint Charles and Auraria were no more. The combined communities now called themselves the Denver City Town Company. Appropriately, William Larimer laid out and named the first streets.

Up in Wyoming, Green Russell heard of the fast-breaking developments around Cherry Creek. Hastily, he assembled another party consisting of twenty-five men. On the way south, they panned virtually every stream between Wyoming and Denver City. Unknown to any of the parties of would-be argonauts, there really was gold here, but it was up in the high Rockies. The first person to figure it out was another southerner, a Missourian named George Jackson, a cousin of Kit Carson. In common with Green Russell, Jackson was a failed veteran of the California excitement. Unlike Easter and Russell, Jackson reasoned that the gold had washed down from the mountains, gravity being what it is. Therefore, the best chance for a fortune was not in the stream beds but in the high country.

Without waiting for warmer weather, Jackson left his camp at Arapahoe City, near present day Golden, for a winter prospecting trip. He chose Clear Creek Canyon, then called the Vasquez Fork, as his route to the high country. Four days of prospecting followed. On the fifth day, he found a promising sand bar and made his camp where West Chicago Creek flows into South Clear Creek, a location that now lies within present-day Idaho Springs. For three days he chopped ice and melted gravel over a huge fire. After finding nuggets of gold, he drew a map before meticulously erasing all signs of his camp. Back at Arapahoe City he passed the winter, keeping his own counsel and confiding only in Tom Golden, whose mouth was as tight as a number two beaver trap.

Following the spring thaw, Jackson returned in early March to work his claim. When supplies ran low, he walked down to Denver City to buy what he needed. Unfortunately, he paid for his purchases in gold dust and nuggets. Word of his affluence spread like measles in a kindergarten. Jackson tried to sneak out of town, but he was powerless to avoid the eager crowd that followed him back to his placer. Eventually, the town of Idaho Springs grew up there as other rich discoveries were made nearby. George Jackson finally sold his claim to a group from Chicago, who gave the name to the creek. Jackson's discovery became one of the reasons for the great gold rush that developed in 1859.

Courtesy State Historical Society of Colorado Library

Here is one of the documented likenesses of John H. Gregory,
discoverer of the great Gregory Mine.

Placer gold, obviously, is not as valuable nor as exciting as the source from which it has been washed down by natural processes of erosion. Called lodes, or veins, these sources are found in rock seams, usually with quartz, where nature put them when the earth was formed. The find was made a scant four months after the Jackson find and less than fifteen miles away, as the crow flies.

It was another Georgian who located it. his name was John Gregory, his hair was red and his vocabulary would have shamed a mule skinner. Gregory's discovery resulted in the emergence of Central City and its several satellites, the principal reason for this book.

2.

JOHN H. GREGORY
AND MOUNTAIN CITY

JOHN GREGORY was just one among several people who had heard of Jackson's good luck. Like Jackson, Gregory was an experienced miner. In 1827, back in Georgia, he had been one of the fortunate ones who had found gold. A non–Indian, he was not expelled, but he went off to California in 1849 anyway. While there he made another rich strike, but he lost everything in the nationwide Panic of 1857. Word of the Canadian discovery at Barkerville on the Frazer River sent Gregory north in 1858. Barkerville was in New Caledonia, now called British Columbia. But Gregory got only as far as Fort Laramie where he worked briefly as a contract hunter, teamster, and did a bit of trapping on the side.

When the rumor of Russell's good luck filtered north, Gregory suddenly lost his enthusiasm for the north country. He chose to investigate the closer prospect instead. He pocketed the day labor money he had saved and turned south. By the time he reached Arapahoe City he was nearly destitute. He stayed with Captain Richard Sopris for about a month. Late in

Collection of Fred and Jo Mazzulla

John H. Gregory of Georgia, first discoverer of gold in
Colorado

Collection of Fred and Jo Mazzulla

The building labeled Gregory Store and one of the homes at the right still stand at Mountain City. Above them are the structures of the Gregory Mine.

Collection of Fred and Jo Mazzulla

The Gregory–Buell Consolidated Gold Mining and Milling Company was located at Mountain City. At the upper right, a train has crossed the trestle, heading up the hill toward Central City.

April he started up Clear Creek with the intention of reaching the Jackson Diggings. As he moved along he worked his gold pan in the gravel, raising enough color to convince himself that a rich lode must be somewhere nearby. Upon reaching the forks of Clear Creek he was in a quandary. Jackson's Diggings was on the south fork, but he was raising better prospects on the north fork. Logically, he trudged up the north fork. Above present Black Hawk his best pans of color led him up a side gulch, now known as Prosser Gulch. It led to his discovery. There on May 6, 1859, Gregory drove his pick into a vein of decomposed quartz, the first discovery of lode gold in the territory.

An unexpected spring blizzard dictated a retreat to the lower settlements. There he waited and kept his own counsel. Eventually his confidence was won over by a band of eager Indiana gold seekers led by Wilkes Defrees. By June contemporary estimates insist that 10,000 men had crowded into the area around Gregory's mine.

Conspicuous among those who came was the crusading editor Horace Greeley and his traveling companion Henry Villard, a noted reporter of the day. Greeley had established the New York Tribune in 1841. Among other causes, he championed land reform, temperance, and the virtues of agriculture as a way of life. Personal honesty was almost a fetish with Horace. When accounts of gold fields in western Kansas Territory reached the East, Greeley was determined to see for himself rather than merely copying the probably inaccurate accounts in competing papers. Being a responsible journalist, he would never print rumors or gossip.

The journey across the prairies was dangerous, but it was an event Greeley never forgot. On May 27, 1859, he boarded a stagecoach of the Leavenworth

This poster encouraged people to ride the Central Overland coaches from St. Joseph to Denver City.

Collection of Freda and Francis Rizzari

Planter's House Hotel stood at the corner of 16th and Blake Streets in Denver. It was built in 1860 as a stagecoach stop and post office. Fire destroyed it in 1875.

and Pikes Peak Express Company at Manhattan, Kansas. Horace considered stagecoaches a threat to his molars. Greeley and Villard stopped for nearly a month in Denver City, which the strait-laced editor soon came to hate. He wrote, "Every other house was a lager beer saloon or a brothel; sometimes both." Some of them sold whiskey, too. The most common variety was Taos Lightning, a coarse New Mexican libation distilled from corn. Pioneers who observed its ingestion noted that those who consumed more than one tin cup of the stuff never lived long enough to become addicted. Another observed that in pioneer Denver City the lightning struck hard, fast, and often.

Collection of Evelyn and Robert L. Brown

Richens Lacy "Uncle Dick" Wootton was the man who brought those barrels of Taos Lightning to pioneer Denver, thus assuring a rowdy Christmas celebration. He also operated the Raton Pass section of the Santa Fe Trail as a toll road.

Collection of Freda and Francis B. Rizzari

This rare envelope was mailed from Mountain City in March of 1862, when Colorado was still a territory.

In mid December of 1858, Richens Lacy "Uncle Dick" Wootton brought the initial barrels of the brew to Denver City in time for the very first celebration of Christmas in the Cherry Creek towns. Possibly the availability of the Wootton's "lightning" had some bearing on the fact that Denver's first Christmas was celebrated with a public wrestling match. Wootton opened Denver City's first saloon. President John Adams wrote, "Saloons are the spawning grounds of disease, vicious habits, bastards, and legislators."

A few of the less scurilous drinking establishments served "Indian Whiskey." Its recipe dated back to the days of Colorado's fur trading posts. It called for a barrel of creek water, two gallons of the cheapest grain alcohol, two ounces of strychnine for the "kick," and three plugs of chewing tobacco for the color and to make the Indians sick. The Native Americans main-

F. KRUSE

GREGORY POINT,

—DEALER IN—

Groceries, Provisions,

TOBACCOS AND CIGARS,

Queen's, Glass, Wooden, Willow and Tinware.

CHOICE TEAS A SPECIALTY.

FRESH BUTTER AND EGGS ALWAYS ON HAND.

Collection of Freda and Francis B. Rizzari

The Kruse Grocery Store was at Gregory Point, a tiny suburb of Mountain City.

tained that if whiskey failed to induce vomiting it was no good. Red pepper was added for the "bite" and a half of a bar of soap gave it a "head." Finally, it was stirred once a day for a week. Then, according to the recipe, one bottle could be swapped for a buffalo robe.

In Denver City's saloons, bartenders were hired according to the size of their thumbs. One drink cost a pinch of gold dust, hence the importance of thumb size. Hard money was in short supply. Quite often a few drinks caused people to listen avidly to Horace Greeley's frequent temperance tirades. Before taking refuge in the Denver House Hotel, Greeley delivered a scathing anti–liquor diatribe inside a saloon. The customers cheered lustily, applauded, and stamped their feet before continuing their drinking. Pioneer Denver was that sort of a place, and the editor was glad to be out of it. With William N. Byers as their guide, the two newsmen boarded Uncle Billy Opdike's stagecoach and were bumped along toward Golden City. After a brief pause to stretch, they abandoned coach travel and made the remaining miles to Central City on mules, arriving on the second day.

Word that the noted editor was to arrive caused a crowd of miners to gather outside the Mountain City log hotel. They noisily demanded a Greeley speech. His oration was a typically political one. He extolled the virtue of motherhood, the flag, and advocated immediate statehood. He castigated the whores and advised his listeners to avoid drinking and gambling.

To assure a favorable press, local boosters salted a dry hole with several shotgun loads of gold dust until the walls fairly glittered. Next morning they offered Horace an opportunity to see for himself how it was done. Within a short span of time the editor had panned out a respectable quantity of the yellow metal. Since he was personally honest, Greeley assumed

Courtesy Gilpin County Museum

This train is rounding the point above Mountain City. Central City is visible ahead of it in the distance.

that others shared the same trait. His published report on the gold mining in the Rocky Mountains was optimistic and gave much encouragement to easterners intent on prospecting beyond the Missouri River.

In the interim, the Russell brothers had returned from Wyoming. What they saw so impressed them that they made one more journey back to Oklahoma, returning with another recently recruited party of prospectors from the South. On their way West, a curious coincidence brought the Russells into contact with a future Gilpin County resident of importance.

Although she had been orphaned at twelve years of age, Mary York had avoided orphanages by working in the Baltimore home of a family named McGee. In

Collection of Nancy and Ed Bathke

This 1867 view of Mountain City was taken by William G. Chamberlain. It looks northeast across the community.

common with many others, the Panic of 1857 left the McGees in dire financial straits. News of gold in Western Kansas seemed to offer a chance for a fresh start. Mary York was their twenty-nine-year-old housemaid. They invited her to come along. Since she had no future prospects, Mary accepted. She was a

Collection of Nancy and Ed Bathke

Packard Gulch's trestle and some of Mountain City's homes
were photographed by Charles Weitfle in 1884.

young lady of meticulous personal habits, and when
they camped by a stream she would wait for darkness
and slip into the water for a quick bath.

One evening while bathing, Mr. McGee and
another man stood near the creek bank. While hiding
herself as best she could, Mary overheard McGee

Courtesy State Historical Society of Colorado Library

Here, stretching up the hillsides above Gregory Gulch, was Mountain City. The view is toward the southwest.

Collection of Evelyn and Robert L. Brown

Here was Mountain City in the winter of 1966.

Collection of James W. Cozens

Former Sheriff William Z. Cozens, his wife Mary York Cozens, and their large family are shown here on the porch of their home in Middle Park.

Collection of Evelyn and Robert L. Brown

The former Cozens' home as it appears today.

Upon retirement, Sheriff Billy Cozens settled with his family on this ranch in Middle Park. Soon a small community grew up around his ranch. When a post office was established there it was called Cozens.

telling how he planned to sell Mary as a prostitute when they reached the Cherry Creek settlements. At first she considered drowning herself, but the Platte River isn't very deep. After supper that night, she gathered her meager personal belongings, crawled out of her tent, and began running. Fortunately, she was picked up, nearly hysterical, by the Russells the following day. She confided in them and they offered her protection.

Mary York stayed with her new friends all the way to the gulch where Green Russell located still another gold placer deposit. Nearby he built a duplex type

Collection of James W. Cozens

Retired Sheriff William Z. Cozens is seen here, seated on the
porch of his home in Middle Park.

Collection of Evelyn and Robert L. Brown

The Cozens' ranch house in Middle Park

Courtesy State Historical Society of Colorado Library

Located halfway between Central City and Black Hawk, Mountain City looked like this when H.H. Lake exposed this picture. Notice the open cut of Gregory's Mine and the train above it, headed for Central City.

log cabin. Mary lived in one side of it and the Russells occupied the other part. It was the first structure in the new town of Russell Gulch, and Mary York was the first lady occupant of the town. She supported herself by baking bread and pastry for the miners. They paid her in gold dust. Among her steady customers was a man named William Z. Cozens, who worked in Kehler's saloon as a bartender and carpenter.

Collection of Evelyn and Robert L. Brown

In this contemporary view, the Gregory Mine, the triangular street plot, and other landmarks are still visible.

Our Civil War dictated that the Russells should return to help defend their native Georgia. After their departure, Mary gave up the duplex and rented a house in Mountain City where she took in boarders and supported herself as a laundress. By saving her earnings she accumulated $225 and bought the house. Billy Cozens became one of Mary York's boarders. One day she asked Billy to build her a dining table with leaves, where she and the boarders could sit to eat. Cozens gave up bartending and began working as a deputy sheriff. At the age of fifty, he was appointed sheriff.

Down in New Mexico, Archbishop Lamy sent Fr. Joseph Projectus Machebeuf north. Following a month on the road, the priest arrived at the Cherry

Creek camps. He regularly conducted services around Denver City, as well as in the towns of Gilpin County. On December 30, 1860, Father Joseph presided at the wedding of Mary York and BIlly Cozens, the first wedding to be performed in the Gregory Mining District.

The discoveries of Russell, Jackson, and Gregory gave substance to what soon became the Pikes Peak Gold Rush. Eastbound travelers, letters written to families in the East, and newspapers spread the news. By the summer of 1859, a deluge of "Fifty-Niners" was crossing the prairies into western Kansas. By June an estimated 10,000 had arrived in the Gregory District. The long anticipated rush was on!

3.

WESTWARD THE GOLD HUNTERS

EARLY IN THE SUMMER OF 1859 accounts of the Russell and Gregory discoveries had filtered eastward. Newspaper dispatches written by both Henry Villard and the highly regarded Horace Greeley fed the public uneasiness of a nation still reeling from the after effects of the Panic of 1857. Disappointed Californians who happened to pass through Fort Laramie or who chanced to return east by way of the Cherry Creek towns carried optimistic reports to their homes in the various eastern states.

A second factor that contributed to the willingness of eastern Americans to move westward was the need for new land in our fundamentally agricultural economy. Such currently accepted practices as contour plowing, crop rotation, or the application of sophisticated fertilizers were practically unknown in the nineteenth century. When a farm consistently failed to produce as it once had, people simply moved on and started over in a different place. And then there was the widely held belief in America's Manifest Destiny.

Among others, Benjamin Franklin and the later presidents Buchanan and Polk embraced the doctrine of Manifest Destiny to rationalize and justify our territorial expansion toward the Pacific Ocean. President James K. Polk was a straitlaced nineteenth century Methodist. His wife was a very strict Presbyterian. During their occupancy of the White House, dancing, card playing, liquor, and tobacco were banned throughout the executive mansion. Sam Houston once remarked, "The trouble with Polk was that he drank too much water."

In the 1840s we annexed Texas, acquired Oregon, and purchased California under a provision of the Treaty of Guadalupe Hidalgo. The doctrine of Manifest Destiny held that God foreordained the expansion of the boundaries of the United States to the western ocean, and possibly beyond. The doctrine had become a popular national belief that spread across the country. It promised a new repository for the increasing millions of people who had crossed the ocean from Europe to escape a variety of tyrannies, real or imagined. Native Americans, Russians on the Pacific Coast, people of Mexican extraction, as well as those who came from England all felt the effects of this popular principle.

To facilitate the westward movement of people, two branches of the Santa Fe Trail as well as the Oregon, California, and Mormon Trails were established. Such explorers as Lewis and Clark, Pike, Gunnison, and Fremont, who mapped and documented the cross-country routes, had all been published. Fremont's journals and maps, written by his wife, Jessie, were commonly accepted as the best and most accurate. For migrants headed for the Pacific Northwest or California, the trails were there. For those who chose the Southwest, the two Santa Fe Roads had been in use since 1821. Although each of these trails was really too far north or south of the

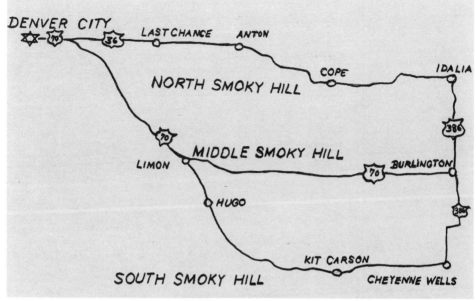

Robert L. Brown

The Smoky Hill Trail

Cherry Creek settlements to be practical, many Fifty-Niners used them on their way to the gold fields of western Kansas. But there was one closer alternative.

Called the Smoky Hill Trail, it followed a route south of the Oregon and north of the Santa Fe Trails, crossing the prairies in a more direct line to Denver City. It paralleled the Republican and Smoky Hill Rivers, utilizing early Plains Indian hunting paths in some places. Thousands of gold seekers, business-men, soldiers, and homesteaders chose this more direct way between 1859 and 1863. There were actually three Smoky Hill Trails, a north, a middle, and a south. All three converged at a point some twelve miles south east of Denver City, the primary western terminus. An accompanying map shows the Smoky Hill roads in relation to current landmarks.

Collection of Evelyn and Robert L. Brown

The foreground ruts are those of the Smoky Hill Trail, still
visible in eastern Arapahoe County

Because it was shorter, the Middle Smoky Hill
Trail was the most popular. It was also the most dangerous. West of the present Kansas–Colorado border
there was very little available water for most of the
year. Due to the loss of life on the Middle Smoky Hill,
greater than on the other two branches combined, it
soon became known as the Starvation Trail. A
reporter for the Rocky Mountain News told of passing
dead bodies beside the trail. Broken wagons and animal bones were common too.

When the sad details of the plight of the Blue
brothers became common knowledge, many people in
Denver City did their "I told you so's." Their party had
originated in Illinois and they opted for a try at the

Middle Smoky Hill Trail. Along the way a few others joined the group. Since water was scarce, so were the wild animals that might have sustained life. When all food supplies were exhausted, they unwisely killed and ate their pack animals. As people died of starvation, their bodies were eaten by the survivors. No one was deliberately killed for food.

The cannibalism occurred about seventy-five miles east of Denver City. Three months later only Daniel Blue survived and made his way into Denver City. Friendly Plains Indians found him, fed him in their village, and helped him reach his destination. Gradually he related the pathetic story. Since he had eaten only the bodies of persons already deceased, including his brother, he was never charged as a murderer. A public subscription of money enabled Daniel to ride a stagecoach back to his native Illinois where he wrote a heart-rending account of his experiences on the Smoky Hill Trail.

As the demand for better transportation accelerated, the Butterfield Overland Dispatch operated an irregular schedule of mule-drawn stagecoaches on the Middle Smoky Hill Road. Beginning on May 7, 1859, Russell, Majors, and Waddell's Leavenworth and Pikes Peak Express Company began running regular daily stagecoaches to the Cherry Creek towns. Each Concord coach accommodated nine very crowded passengers for the six day journey. Many who were able to pay the $125 fare brought along large quantities of liquor to soften the bone-shattering ride.

Russell, Majors, and Waddell built twenty-seven "Mile Houses" between Leavenworth, Kansas, and Denver City. Here, emigrants could purchase badly prepared food while fresh animals were being harnessed to the coach. All of the Mile Houses were named for the distances out of Denver. The Four Mile

House still stands in a Denver park on South Forest Street. The last stagecoaches on the Smoky Hill Trail came into Denver City in June of 1866. Those gold seekers who could not afford the $125 fare sometimes walked the entire 900 miles from Leavenworth.

Upon arrival, the people faced a peculiar political situation, but few of them really cared about such things, until forced to do so. For instance, most of the mining region, including Denver and Central City, was still a part of Arapahoe County, Kansas. Boulder City was within Nebraska. At this time, the fortieth parallel (which is now the Baseline Road through Boulder) separated Kansas and Nebraska. Breckenridge was a part of Utah Territory while much of present-day southern Colorado was within New Mexico Territory.

The first attempt in Congress to create a Colorado Territory was a failure. Frustrated residents of the region felt neglected and drew up an illegal constitution of their own on October 24, 1859, creating Jefferson Territory. A constitution was adopted and officials were elected. Judge Robert W. Steele of the town of Mount Vernon was chosen to be governor.

Mail delivery from home was a problem too, until the Pony Express relayed the first letters for Central City and Denver from Julesburg in April of 1860. Julesburg was the only Pony Express station in Colorado. On February 28, 1861, Congress finally created Colorado Territory, appropriating land from Kansas, Nebraska, New Mexico, and Utah Territories. It was divided into seventeen counties. President Buchanan signed the proclamation, one of the few popular acts of this beleaguered executive. Eleven thousand, eight hundred and thirty-seven foot high Buchanan Pass crosses the Continental Divide north of Central City and south of Rocky Mountain National

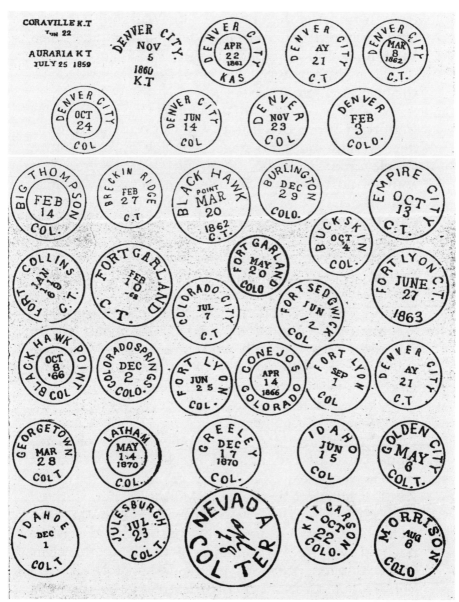

Collection of Evelyn and Robert L. Brown

Early Colorado Postmarks, 1859-1876

The earliest postmarks designate the area as Kansas Territory. C.T. is an abbreviation for Colorado Territory, created in February 28, 1861.

Park. It remains the only place in Colorado that honors President Buchanan. President Lincoln succeeded Buchanan and appointed his friend, William Gilpin, to be the first territorial governor. Central City became the seat of Gilpin County.

For new arrivals to travel the thirty-four miles from the Cherry Creek towns to Central City, a journey by mule-back or stagecoach lay ahead. Horace Greeley rode a coach as far as Golden City, then transferred to a mule for the remaining distance. A modest distance west of Denver City there were three supply towns, located along the base of the foothills. Their names were Mount Vernon, Apex, and Golden Gate City. Food, clothing, and mining supplies were for sale in each of the three towns. In each instance, a trail of sorts led up into the mountains. Any one of the three trails provided access to Central City.

Mount Vernon stood next to the point where Colorado Highway 93 passes beneath Interstate Highway 70. Although its site is now covered by a landfill, the Matthews–Winters Historic Park commemorates the location. Judge Robert W. Steele was the governor of the illegal Jefferson Territory. A monument marks the site of his cabin. George Morrison's stone house still stands. Its access trail was named the Denver City, Mount Vernon, and Gregory Toll Road. It followed the spine of Mount Vernon Canyon somewhat below the lanes of Interstate 70. At a place called Hayward's Junction a branch road turned north down the steep grades of Big Hill into Clear Creek Canyon, then up to the forks of North and South Clear Creek. Beyond that point the road followed North Clear Creek as far as Black Hawk, then up the hill into Central City.

Big Hill was a precipitous grade. Drivers used a block and tackle, with one end tied to a stout tree and

This drawing of the supply town of Mount Vernon looks westward up the canyon.

the other to the rear axle. Some teamsters merely wrapped the rope around the tree trunk and let friction snub the wagon down. Friction burns left by the braking ropes are visible to this day to hikers on the grades of Big Hill. Tree bark has now grown over the wounds, but distinct indentations still remain. Since a tree grows from the stalk out and from the top up, the scars are visible at eye level.

Barely north of Mount Vernon was the town of Apex, now buried beneath the landfill that supports a miniature train at the Heritage Square amusement park. A second town, also know as Apex, appeared in 1891 in Gilpin County's Pine Creek Mining district. It

Collection of Freda and Francis Rizzari

Golden Gate City was the supply town at the mouth of Golden Gate Canyon. A camera obscura was probably responsible for this likeness.

should not be confused with the earlier community. From Apex, the supply town, the migrant trail was named the Apex and Gregory Toll Road. It ascended the steep brush-filled gulch directly behind the little train. Although Apex is gone, the trail is still there and walkers can hike for a couple of miles above the amusement park. It is well marked to guide the interested hiker.

Easily the most direct of the roads to Central City was the Golden Gate and Gregory Toll Road, incorporated in 1862. It followed Golden Gate Canyon from the supply town of Golden Gate City. Its toll gate stood barely west of the junction of the canyon road with Colorado State Highway 93. Golden Gate City existed because of the toll gate, and grew up around it. In common with Mount Vernon and Apex, Golden Gate City no longer exists. However, each spring, preferably in late April, it is still possible to see the scar of the town's principal street before the grass turns green. The best viewpoint is on North Table Mountain late in the afternoon when the shadows are long.

Originally, the grade of the toll road was somewhat above the present twisting road up the canyon to Golden Gate State Park. Where the road intersects with Colorado State Highway 119, it was just a short jaunt downhill to Black Hawk, then up Gregory Gulch to Central City. The first road did not go upward through Golden Gate Canyon. When Gregory returned to his mine he did not travel through Golden Gate Canyon as it was too narrow at the time. Instead, he traversed the first gulch to the north and came down close to the future site of the Eight Mile House. This trail lasted only two or three months.

At one time it was possible to cross Guy Hill, then over Dory and Silver Hills before dropping directly down into Black Hawk. For several months this latter approach became the most used by would-be miners. However, the steepness of Dory Hill, plus many accidents, caused a shift to Golden Gate Canyon's more gradual grades. Incidentally, Mr. E. W. Henderson had the distinction of bringing in the first wagon that was ever snubbed down the precipitous declivities of the so-called Old Gregory Trail. The golden Gate Canyon Toll Road was not open for travel until a month or two later. That twenty yoke of oxen were required to hall in a small boiler suggests the character of those first roads.

Collection of Evelyn and Robert L. Brown

West of Golden, this now empty meadow was the former site of Golden Gate City. Now, only the mountains look the same.

Golden Gate City, as well as the canyon, was supposedly named for the golden riches above it at Central City and in the several surrounding towns mushrooming around it. Quite logically, the entire complex took on the official name of the Gregory Mining District. Both miners and local boosters referred to it as the Richest Square Mile on Earth. Down through the years Gilpin County has been Colorado's most stable mining area, having survived several mild declines without completely closing down. Although its production never approached that of Cripple Creek, Gilpin County continued to turn out gold and other minerals for a longer span of years. Central City has always retained a small population and has avoided becoming a ghost town.

4.

THE EARLY DAYS IN CENTRAL CITY

AT FIRST IT WAS KNOWN AS CENTRE CITY, but residents chose to call it Central City because of its central location between John Gregory's Mine at Mountain City and the rich properties up above it in Nevada Gulch. Currently, it claims to be Colorado's oldest surviving mountain community. Actually, San Luis in Colorado's southern mountains is older.

By June of 1859, between 10,000 and 15,000 eager men had crowded into Gregory Gulch. Some had come up by ox or mule-drawn wagons, others rode horses or mules, a few pushed hand carts and the rest were pedestrians. Each day the air grew thicker with dust from the digging and smoke from blasting powder. When Horace Greeley showed up in June of 1859, he noted that there were about a hundred log cabins and tiny shanties under construction, with three or four times more in the planning stage. Greeley also recorded that most of the people slept in tents and cooked over open fires. He expressed his doubts that any real tables or chairs existed anywhere in the new town. Somewhat to the chagrin of the straitlaced Horace, some of the dirt floored tents were

Collection of Freda and Francis Rizzari

This somewhat grainy 1859 picture from the *Mining Investor* may be the earliest picture in this book. The view is to the north, along Main Street.

crude saloons dispensing powerful Taos Lightning for a fifty-cent pinch of gold dust per tin cup.

When John Gregory returned on May 6, he brought along eleven companions to see his claim. Two yokes of oxen and some pack animals transported the provisions supplied by David K. Wall, a mer-

Collection of Nancy and Ed Bathke

This early Central City view is from half of a stereo pair. Note the big rock outcropping at left and the Teller House at far right.

Collection of Evelyn and Robert L. Brown

From the same place, the rock outcropping is still there. So is the Teller House.

chant at Golden Gate City. Although ice and snow still covered Gregory's claim, Destiny herself had opened her arms at last. Henry Villard, Greeley's companion, wrote that Gregory had already extracted $1,100 worth of gold in his first four days of work. Among Gregory's companions, the Ziegler brothers realized $2,030 in five days while Wilkes De Frees and his brother got $1,522 from three nearby claims in just six days. Several others in Gregory's party also did well.

On June 24, William Newton Byers, founder and editor of the *Rocky Mountain News,* hurried over from Jackson's Diggings in company with five other reporters. After they had pitched their tents, Dr. Joseph Casto took Byers to interview Gregory, who showed them a crudely retorted two pound ball of gold. One account tells how the gold was hidden beneath a Dutch oven upon which Gregory was seated. He held a rifle across his knees as the men conversed. Allegedly, Gregory kept repeating, "Now my wife can be a lady and my children can be schooled."

Soon after the Byers interview, Gregory sold his mine for $21,000 and announced that he was now available as a prospector for other people at a stipend of $200 a day: a princely sum in a troubled economy where ten dollars a week was a typical salary. When a large percentage of his locations became fine gold producing properties, no one was more surprised than John Gregory. Truly, this was the richest square mile on earth. Understandably, each new find enhanced his reputation, but the time came when the discoverer decided to quit while he was ahead. By all reports he was homesick for Georgia and his family. Gregory made his way back home and did not return to Central City until April of 1861.

Collection of Nancy and Ed Bathke

This Co-Op View Company photo looks east over lower
Central City.

Because John Gregory had feared theft, there is
one story that editor Byers took pity on him and vol-
unteered to take the crudely retorted gold through to
Omaha for safe keeping. With only one spare driver,
the gold was delivered to Omaha in just twelve days.
When a bank placed Gregory's samples on public view
in its front window, doubts suddenly vanished.
Almost overnight the word spread to the East and the
rush to the golden gulch was on.

To cope with the inevitable horde of thieves, claim jumpers, sluice box raiders, and murderers that had caused Gregory and others to arm themselves, a mining district was hastily formed. Mining districts consisted of a few common sense rules to protect people where no other laws existed. The first were the jurisdictional invention of the original California Forty-Niners. They stipulated how large a claim could be, how may claims per man would be permitted, and the amount of work one must perform to qualify for and hold a title.

Three types of claims were allowed. A mountain claim would be 50 by 100 feet in size. Gulch claims measured 100 feet, extending from bank to bank. Creek or placer claims could be 100 feet square. In Gregory Gulch each man was allowed one of each type of claim. For those who claimed to be permanent, a ranch claim was also recognized. Building claims in the emerging town allowed forty feet of frontage by 100 feet in depth. All water claims were held as real estate and were not "jumpable."

But the early settlers soon realized claim size regulations alone were not a viable deterrent to crime. For instance, what could or should they do with those who broke the rules? The nearest courts were hundreds of miles away in Kansas City (Westport) or Omaha. So the miners followed the example of prospectors on other frontiers and assembled a body of their own rules of criminal law, covering the most flagrant offenses against good taste.

There were, they decided, four classifications of crime that warranted punishment. For petit larceny, a fine equal to double the amount stolen would be assessed. If a jury was so inclined, extra punishment could be prescribed. Grand larceny carried the same penalties, plus no more than 300 lashes to be administered at the public whipping post. Public punishment of one sort or another came across from Great Britain with the earliest settlers. Whipping was common in the Massachusetts Bay colony and at colonial Williamsburg, Virginia. Denver City had a whipping post. "Noisy Tom" Pollock was both the whipper and the hangman. Persons found guilty of grand larceny were also subject to banishment from the district.

Manslaughter and theft of a horse or mule usually resulted in a public trial in a miners' court. Judges, like preachers, traveled a regular circuit. Usually the judge came to Central City once each month. Miners' court trials were often held in saloons because they offered the largest room in town. Juries consisted of whoever was drinking in the place at the time, assuming that they were sober enough to render judgment. In his first book, *Roughing It,* Mark Twain wrote about a miners' court he had observed in Virginia City. All deliberations and a hanging in the alley behind the saloon were accomplished in just over half an hour. Twain said that he had never before seen a court with so little nonsense about it in his life. A miner's court could assess a verdict of whipping, banishment, or hanging.

The fourth and most serious crime was murder. Here the penalty was a public hanging. In one of the side gulches above Central City there is a large tree that was supposedly used for this purpose. Many early pictures of public hangings have survived. One taken at Leadville's fairground shows the hanged bodies of two men in front of a suspended sheet of canvas, to improve visibility. Many well-dressed spectators, some with picnic baskets in their wagons, are in the foreground.

Judge Isaac C. Parker, the so-called hanging judge, once said, "The certainty of punishment halts

The above are examples of short beer checks or trade tokens used in Central City to stimulate trade and to assist in making change.

crime." Parker sentenced 168 people to death. Of this total, eighty-eight men and seven women were hanged by his "Local Uplift Society." At times Parker acted as his own hangman.

When Colorado became a territory in 1861 both miners' courts and people's courts were abolished. Better qualified judges were assigned to ride the circuits. Typical of those who rode the circuits was Judge Allen Bradford of Central City. Judge Bradford presided over the trials in Gilpin County and its environs. Eventually he was sent to Washington as the territory's non-voting representative in Congress. Bradford was a small man with a squeaky voice, the subject of a number of humorous anecdotes.

Courtesy State Historical Society of Colorado Library

When the brass rail in front of the bar was still in place, and before the Face on the Barroom Floor was painted, the Teller House bar looked like this.

All of the forms of punishment, whipping, banishment, and hanging, had economy in common. Every family wagon had a whip in the front socket, and a rope beneath the seat in case they got stuck in the mud. Banishment required only a firearm and a few moments. In the early years most who came to Colorado hoped to make a quick fortune and return home. Why spend money on juries, sheriffs, or probation officers? But Central City became a permanent community with a jail and a sheriff, the efficient William Z. Cozens.

By the end of autumn, the easy to recover surface gold was playing out. There was still plenty of rich ore,

Collection of Evelyn and Robert L. Brown.

Charles Weitfle took this picture sometime in the 1870s. Its view is toward the east. The two story building at the far right is the soft drink Bottle House.

but it was located deep beneath the surface, and deep mining is not a poor man's game. As winter approached, the summer miners drifted over to Boulder, down to Denver City, or to the lower elevations of the piedmont supply towns. Central City's

Collection of Nancy and Ed Bathke

This early view of the Central City School was taken by Reed and McKenney, who had a Denver studio in 1871 and 1872.

population declined to about a thousand persons who elected to remain.

A number of those who stayed were men of foresight and experience who had located promising deep gold locations: men who had recognized a good spot, kept quiet about it, and stayed where they were. Gradually, a slow but orderly growth began to be evident. Central City became the leading community in Gregory Gulch.

Since the cost of transporting raw ores to refineries sometimes exceeded the value of the gold,

Professor Nathaniel P. Hill, of Brown University, built a stamp mill at Black Hawk. Some of Central City's mines turned out refractory (difficult to refine) ores. Prior to this time only the mills at Swansea in far-off Wales had been able to successfully extract gold from refractory rock. Professor Hill solved the problem. He traveled incognito to Swansea and secured work in their smelter until he had mastered the process. Upon returning to Black Hawk, he established the Boston and Colorado Smelter in 1867, enabling many closed properties to reopen and operate at a profit.

During its second year of life Central City had introduced a summer theatrical season. The theater, plus the later Opera House and a school, acted as cultural magnets, thus enabling the city to become the

Collection of Evelyn and Robert L. Brown

Central City's Miller Block was erected in 1874. It has housed a variety of businesses including a saloon, fruit store, and several others. Currently it is a casino.

leading business center and mainstay of the area's prosperity.

Colorado Territory was finally created, emerging during the 1861–65 years of our Civil War. Approximately half of the population had come out from the South, and many of them were deeply loyal to the Confederacy. In Denver City a Confederate flag was raised in front of the Murphy and Wallingford store. Along toward evening a group of Northern sympathizers finally got their act together, stormed the place and "ripped down the rag of treason." In Black Hawk a Southern flag appeared on a pole at one of the mills. As in Denver, an angry mob tore it down. Only quick action by Sheriff Cozens averted a tragedy.

By December of 1861, men were leaving the gulch in modest numbers to return East and enlist in the armed forces of their choice. Southerners who stayed were often shunned. A Confederate newspaper, *The Mountaineer,* was published for a time in Central City. Its editor feuded editorially with William Newton Byers' pro–Union *Rocky Mountain News.*

The national election of 1860 held far-reaching significance for the people who had come out to find gold. That year the Democratic Party was split between Stephen Douglas and John C. Breckinridge. Unable to resolve their dilemma, they fielded two tickets. Predictably, the result was a disastrous split in the electoral vote that made it possible for the candidate of the infant Republican Party to slip into office with a scant forty percent of the vote. Abraham Lincoln was a minority president, not a unanimous choice of the people. Once in office it became his duty to select the territorial officials. William Gilpin, Lincoln's close friend, became the first territorial governor. Gilpin was a man of strong Northern sentiments. He had accompanied the explorer John C.

Collection of Lewis Carter

This lengthy parade is marching along Spring Street.
Question: Why is the grandstand empty? Is everyone in the parade?

Collection of Evelyn and Robert L. Brown

Here is present Spring Street. Many of the structures shown in the parade picture still exist.

Courtesy State Historical Society of Colorado Library

Among other things, Gilpin County, the town of Gilpin, Gilpin Street, and Gilpin School were all named for William Gilpin, Colorado's first territorial governor.

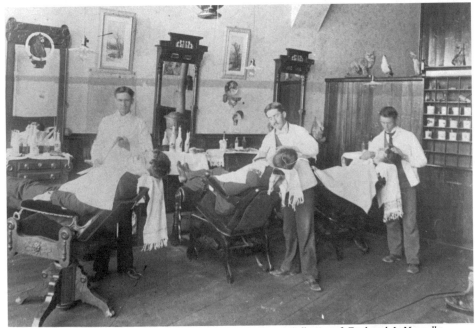

Collection of Fred and Jo Mazzulla

Here was a Central City barber shop. Notice that the chairs are not fastened to the floor. When a barber moved he took his chair. Also observe the personalized shaving mugs at the far right.

Fremont in the 1840s and had learned to love the West. Lincoln also chose Gilpin to be one of his personal bodyguards on the train trip from Springfield to Washington.

Upon his arrival in Colorado, Governor Gilpin stood on the balcony of the Tremont House Hotel and delivered a ringing endorsement of the Union side of the question. His speech took Denver by surprise and nobody even took a shot at him.

William Gilpin remained a carefree bachelor until the age of fifty-nine. Long after the war, he met a St. Louis widow, Julia Pratt Dickerson, and married her in 1874. Mrs. Dickerson had a positive genius for cre-

Collection of Fred and Jo Mazzulla

Colorado's oldest apothecary shop was on Eureka Street in Central City.

ating domestic uproar. Ever after, it was said the governor had a harried look, never knowing where it was coming from next. Today, Gilpin Street, Gilpin School, Gilpin County, and the ghost town of Gilpin still bear his name.

Samuel F. Tappan, owner of a hardware store in Central City, was another intensely partisan champion of the Union cause. As his time permitted, he recruited mountain men for service in the First Colorado Cavalry. As a reward for his efforts Governor Gilpin commissioned Tappan a Lieutenant Colonel. When news of the Confederate plan (to march north from Texas to capture Colorado's gold mines) reached Central City, Tappan and Captain Richard Sopris, also of Central City, joined the First Regiment of

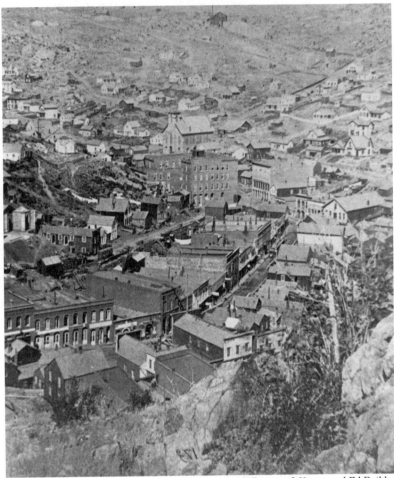

Collection of Nancy and Ed Bathke

This overview of Central City was taken by the Duhem Brothers, who had a Denver studio between 1869 and 1879. St. James Methodist Church and the Teller House can be seen near the picture's center.

Colorado Volunteers and marched south to New Mexico.

Colonel John Slough, a Denver attorney and Major John M. Chivington, presiding elder of Colorado's Methodists, led the Volunteers in three

Collection of Louis Carter

Two groups, the Rough and Ready and the Rescuers posed in front of the Armory–Fire Department building

spectacular fights around Glorieta Pass. Under Chivington's leadership, the Colorado men won three glorious victories and the Texans returned home—on foot.

Meanwhile, the economy of Central City fluctuated with each Northern success or failure. Most Coloradans feared an attack by Southern sympathizers who still lived here. Central City's gold could buy many of the weapons of war from the sympathetic British, if the financially strapped Confederacy could just get their hands on it. There were also rumors, probably originating in the South, that resentful Indians would join the Confederates and lay waste to

Collection of Evelyn and Robert L. Brown

Central City's Fire Department was housed in the Armory Hall. The building is still there. It was recently purchased as the site for a casino.

Colorado towns. Fortunately, neither of these fears materialized.

One of the more tragic aspects of the misunderstandings between the North and South was that neither side realized, until it was too late, that the other side was desperately earnest. Both Abraham Lincoln and Jefferson Davis recognized the value of the West's gold deposits and what their possession could mean to their respective causes. If the Confederate invasion of New Mexico succeeded, who can say how long the war might have continued?

Consequently, the South mounted two other efforts to capture the output of Colorado's mines.

Collection of Leo and Mitzi Stambaugh

This rare photograph shows Central City in the 1880s. It was taken from the Colorado Central Railroad grade, at the point where it curves left toward the depot. Notice the tracks in the lower left foreground.

Later in 1862, the same year of the Glorieta Pass fights, two Denver men of pro–Confederate leanings, decided to try it once more. William P. McClure was Denver's postmaster. Charles Harrison was the proprietor of the rowdy and lawless Criterion Saloon. Somehow they were able to sell the idea that an attack from the east would be less suspect and might succeed. An armed party assembled and crossed Kansas, but a band of Osage Indians saw them and recognized a chance to acquire contraband goods. A running fight ensued, resulting in total extermination of the southerners. Scalping followed the usual pattern until they reached Harrison's body. Harrison was bald. Following a conference, the Osage took his beard instead.

Two years later, in 1864, the final effort fizzled up in South Park. Jim and John Reynolds, ex–southerners who resided in Fairplay, assembled a party of twenty-five for a guerrilla type raid. They robbed a $40,000 gold shipment on a McLaughlin Brothers stagecoach at a point near present Como. Four posses assembled to pursue them. Following a running fight, the bandits divided their loot. Some escaped. The valley route they followed is still a matter of debate, resulting in Colorado's best buried treasure story. Geneva Creek, Hall Valley, Scot Gomer Creek, Deer Creek, and Handcart Gulch all abut on the Continental Divide. Presumably the gold was hastily buried, some of it anyway. Years later, $18,000 was recovered from a mine shaft south of Fairplay. The *Fairplay Flume* for April 18, 1906, contains details. The rest of the money has never been found.

Following the end of hostilities, both Sam Tappan and Richard Sopris returned home as heroes. By 1865, Central City's population had started to climb until some 5,000 persons lived there by the end of the year. It had now become a law-abiding place where families with children made their homes. In the early 1870s, Central City became the official seat of Gilpin County, with a population greater than Denver's.

5.

CENTRAL CITY'S SATELLITES

IN NEARLY ALL OF COLORADO'S more prosperous mining areas, there was usually one of the larger communities that emerged as the leading cultural and supply center. In Lake County it was Leadville. Cripple Creek became the most important place in Teller County. In Park County it was Fairplay, while in Gilpin County, Central City quickly assumed dominance. In almost all cases a cluster of smaller satellite villages grew up around the dominant town. In some instances a dependent town might also achieve permanence, but most did not survive.

Colorado's Gregory Gulch area held a number of other communities too. Most of them were small. Mountain City was important because it was the site of Gregory's mine. The first religious services conducted in the district were at Mountain City on June 12. The "city" also had a tent hotel, a Masonic Temple, a log-walled theater, and about 200 cabins. Its thoroughfares climbed, street over street, up the steep hillsides on both sides of the gulch. At one time Mountain City sported a weekly newspaper, but its life span was short. Subscribers insisted that its name was so lengthy that after they had digested it there

This unusual view looks across Gregory Gulch at Mountain
City. The trestle appears at the upper right.

was little time left for news items. It was called *The
Rocky Mountain Gold Reporter and Rocky Mountain
Herald.* Publication was suspended in October of
1860. Mountain City was the second town established
in the Gregory District. It boasted that its Masonic
Lodge was the first in the mountains, but it was not
chartered until the end of 1861. Inevitably, Central
City absorbed Mountain City in the 1870s.

Bortonsburg was in Illinois Gulch, west of
Missouri City. It, too, had a short life span. In common with Mountain City it had a hotel, but its hotel
was in a permanent building. Wilkes Defrees, who
brought a party of gold seekers from Indiana, started

Collection of Fred and Jo Mazzulla

From a point just above Pine Street is a view of Gregory Gulch, looking downhill toward Mountain City and Black Hawk. The steeple of St. Mary's of the Assumption Church appears at the right.

Collection of Evelyn and Robert L. Brown

From the same viewpoint, many original structures are still visible, including St. Mary's of the Assumption Church.

This Duhem Brothers photo was taken of Nevadaville in 1870
or 1872.

the Bortonsburg Hotel. Only partial foundations now
mark the town's location.

Wilkes Defrees started another hotel in Hoosier
City. (The town took its name from the Hoosier state
of Indiana.) Horace Greeley mentioned the hotel in
one of his dispatches. Greeley spent some time in

Collection of Nancy and Ed Bathke

Photographer Ed Tangen exposed this panoramic view of Russell Gulch. The Methodist Church shows on the upper street.

Hoosier City prior to his speech to the miners' meeting. Hoosier City declined after a couple of months when Defrees returned to Indiana.

Springfield was a tiny collection of cabins located in Spring Gulch. Eureka was in Eureka Gulch, approximately a half mile west of Central City. Hughesville was different. It was a silver mining camp situated on Silver Mountain, northeast of Black Hawk. At times Missouri City was known as Missouri Flats. Established just a few miles southwest of

Central City, Missouri City had hoped to interest the Leavenworth and Pikes Peak Express Company in establishing their terminus within the settlement. The express company refused the offer and the town diminished soon thereafter. Only its tiny cemetery still remains.

Gregory Point was situated at the place where Eureka, Nevada, and Spring Creeks come together. Mammoth City, another small camp, was in Mammoth Gulch, over the pass west of Apex. It was once described by a local optimist as, "the center of the Gilpin County or Central City Gold Belt." Its reason for existing was the Centennial and German Tunnels drilled into Mammoth Hill. All of these short-lived settlements were within a five mile radius of Central City. Several of them had considered merging into each other.

But there were three other communities within the vicinity that grew larger, had substantial populations, and prospered for several years. One of the three, Black Hawk, is still a thriving town claiming about 300 permanent residents. The other two were Russell Gulch and Nevadaville.

Horace Greeley aptly described the assorted settlements in Gregory Gulch as "resembling the rungs on a ladder, with one town above the other, so close together that differentiating between them is difficult." At the base of the ladder is Black Hawk, which grew up at the lower end of the gulch where it abuts North Clear Creek. Its name came from a quartz mill erected there in May of 1860. The mill's manufacturer was the Black Hawk Company of Rock Island, Illinois. The company was named for the Sac and Fox Indian Chief and the town simply kited the name of the mill. At one time Chief Black Hawk was in Arapahoe City with Gregory.

Collection of Evelyn and Robert L. Brown

This early view of Black Hawk looks up Gregory Street at the left. Chase Gulch is at the far right. At the lower right is Nathaniel Hill's Boston and Colorado Smelter. Black Hawk's school and Presbyterian Church are at left of center.

Collection of Evelyn and Robert L. Brown

From the same angle, here is contemporary Black Hawk. Many original landmarks are still visible.

Collection of Nancy and Ed Bathke

Nathaniel P. Hill, standing in the doorway, built his Boston and Colorado Smelter at Black Hawk. Metallurgist Richard Pearce is at left. The stacked silver bricks, worth $45,000, are the ingots President Grant walked across at the Teller House.

A number of Colorado towns went through a series of name changes, but Black Hawk never did, although it was known as Blackhawk between 1895 and 1950. The Lee brothers and a man named Judd supposedly laid out the town.

Collection of Nancy and Ed Bathke

This interior view of Black Hawk's Bobtail Mine was taken by a photographer for the Keystone View Company in 1898. The Bobtail was sold for $100,000.

Colorado's Territorial Legislature incorporated Black Hawk as a city in March of 1864. Unlike other Gregory district towns, it was never noted for its mines, although geologists insist there are rich ore bodies nearby. For most of its years Black Hawk's ready water supply dictated that it should be a milling and refining town. Early photographs show an

Collection of Nancy and Ed Bathke

Charles Weitfle took this view of Black Hawk. It shows the railroad tracks and the cover over Clear Creek, looking toward the north.

impressive number of these facilities erected in the lower part of the town, along the edge of North Clear Creek. Ores from the several rich properties above Black Hawk were carted down the hill for refinement where the needed water was plentiful.

Collection of Nancy and Ed Bathke

Joseph Collier took this view of Black Hawk. Note that Clear Creek has been covered over to make room for the railroad tracks.

But the water that brought prosperity was also the cause of one of the town's most vexing problems. People in nineteenth century Colorado knew almost nothing about environmental damage. Consequently, the upper watersheds of the gulch were gradually stripped of the trees needed to build homes and shore up mine shafts. With little to hold back moisture from melting spring snow packs that fed the flood's insatiable appetite for soil and shrubs, Gregory Gulch sometimes became a raging torrent of mud and water. Spring floods rushed downhill through Black Hawk and into North Clear Creek. One flash flood in the early 1860s washed away the First Methodist Church from Swede Hill. Finally a flume was installed down one side of the street and covered over by a plank sidewalk that is still visible. At one time the entire creek was covered.

Black Hawk's principal street follows the narrow contour of the gulch. Quite logically it was named Gregory Street. It continues uphill past the Bobtail Mine to the remains of Mountain City. Beyond that point it continues uphill to the remains of Mountain City. There Gregory Street branches off to the left to end at Main Street. Just above Mountain City the principal road up the gulch becomes Lawrence Street. Finally, at the junction of Main and Lawrence Streets, the main thoroughfare becomes Eureka Street as it climbs through Central City to the cemeteries near the top of the hill. There were three burial grounds at the head of Eureka Gulch, and the hill leading to them is steep enough to give rise to grisly humor.

One of the favorite stories tells of a casket being hauled up to the cemetery. On the steepest grade the coffin slid backwards, dropped out of the tailgate, and began sliding down through Central City to Gregory Street and into Black Hawk. There it entered the doorway of the local drug store. Striking the counter, the casket upended and the lid opened. It happened that the clerk was quite nearsighted. He looked at the corpse with a squint and asked, "May I help you sir?"

To which the man in the box replied, "Please give me something to stop this awful coffin!"

When the lecturer and traveler Bayard Taylor toured the Gregory District in 1866 he described Black Hawk's "charming church, [Presbyterian] perched above the town on the extremity of the headland [Bates Hill] that separates Gregory Gulch from Clear Creek." The Black Hawk church was built in 1863. As for the town itself, Taylor wrote that it was, "a busy, noisy, and thickly populated region. The puff of steam, the dull thump of the stamp mills and all of the other machinery at work filled the air." Bayard Taylor's description of Gregory Street portrayed it as "a rough, winding, dusty road, lined with crowded wooden buildings; hotels with pompous names and limited accommodations; drinking saloons, bakeries, log and frame dwelling houses, piles of rusty and useless machinery tumbled by the wayside. There was also a brewery. In the center of the gulch a stream of muddy water rushed downhill."

Black Hawk's population rose to about 2,000 in the early 1870s. Except for the narrowness of the canyon it might have grown larger. Its cemetery on Dory Hill was the first in the state. The Hendrie Brothers established Colorado's first mining machinery foundry west of the Teller House. Black Hawk also had the district's first jail.

On the south side of Gregory Street between Black Hawk and Mountain City was the previously mentioned Bobtail Tunnel, which cuts vertically across several rich gold veins. Its unusual name came from the story of the initial lode of ore, transported to the sluice by an ox with a closely cropped tail. The animal had been harnessed to a forked tree limb with an animal hide stretched across it. One very proper lady staunchly refused to say, "Bobtail." She continu-

Collection of Frances and Richard Ronzio

Black Hawk's Toll Gate Saloon stood on the west side of Clear
Creek. One of the "ladies of the eveing" is seated in an upstairs
window.

ally referred to the property as the "Robert
Appendage." Initially, the Bobtail Tunnel was drilled
to drain off underground water, making access to the
gold veins easier. Relays of mules hauled the loaded

Collection of Evelyn and Robert L. Brown

In August of 1914 a flood came down Gregory Street in Black Hawk. A large culvert beneath the sidewalk precludes a recurrence. Notice two of "the girls" in the second floor bay window.

Collection of Evelyn and Robert L. Brown

This contemporary view matches the flood photograph, minus the "ladies of the evening."

Collection of Evelyn and Robert L. Brown

T.H. Crook is referred to in some accounts as Thorvald Crook.
In others he is listed as Tom. His Crook's Palace Saloon occupied at least two locations. The present Crook's Palace survives as a restaurant, casino, and bar. The tokens shown are
short beer checks from Crook's.

ore cars to the surface until an electric tram line was completed, enabling the ores to be moved down and dumped directly into bins at the mill.

Each evening during its boom years, Black Hawk became a rip-roaring place with many saloons and gambling dens. Sometimes both would be under the same roof. The infamous Toll Gate Saloon was one such place. A drinking establishment, billiard room, and gambling hall occupied the first floor. "Ladies of the evening" were available in the upstairs rooms. One of them is visible, in a second floor window in one of the photographs included in this chapter. In a second picture two of "the girls" are looking out of a second story window while one of Black Hawk's periodic floods rages down Gregory Street.

Typical of Black Hawk's thirst quenchers was Crook's Palace, also located on Gregory Street. Thorvald H. Crook built the original structure. It was a two story frame building with a skylight. Crook demolished it around the turn of the century and had the present Crook's Palace, of brick construction, built at the same site, on the south side of Gregory Street. Today it survives as one of Black Hawk's casinos.

There was a quieter side to Black Hawk's social life also. In winter, people came from the surrounding towns to join the parties held regularly at the ice skating rink, the only such facility in the district. Bobsled parties were popular too. For those brave enough to try it, the course or run started up in Nevadaville. Riders on the sleds sped down a 500-foot drop in elevation within the first two miles. As their velocity increased, they sped through Central City, Mountain City, and down into Black Hawk. Frightened pedestrians and upset mule-drawn wagons were regarded as a part of the fun. In view of the steep final pitch of

Collection of Fred and Jo Mazzulla

In its heyday, Black Hawk's Gilpin Hotel was a well known hostelry, complete with a dining room. Despite a recent fire, the building still stands.

Gregory Street and its abrupt end at the North Fork of Clear Creek, how did the sledders manage to stop? The alternative to the creek was a sheer canyon wall. Thus far no one has been able to explain how it was accomplished.

Each spring there were house dances (supervised, of course) and card parties. Summer weather

Collection of Evelyn and Robert L. Brown

Black Hawk's old Gilpin Hotel is now a gambling casino. This view was taken in 1974.

brought moonlight picnics, lager beer parties, and dancing under the stars at Lemkuhl's Brewery Garden. Boating was popular at Lake House in Lake Gulch. Each autumn when Gilpin County's deciduous trees changed color, there were leaf-peeping picnics in the aspen groves.

Green Russell had suspected for a long time that the first gold he had placered out at the junction of Dry Creek and the South Platte River had washed down from the mountains. He prospected up the drainage of Clear Creek to check out his suspicions. He found its source in Russell Gulch, the site of his second discovery of placer gold. Russell Gulch, the town, is located on a parallel creek, a couple of miles

Collection of Evelyn and Robert L. Brown

Black Hawk's Cracker Works appears at the lower right in this picture. A Colorado Central train appears to be parked on the trestle over Gregory Street.

Collection of Nancy and Ed Bathke

Driving near Russell Gulch, according to this somewhat sylized postcard, must have been quaint.

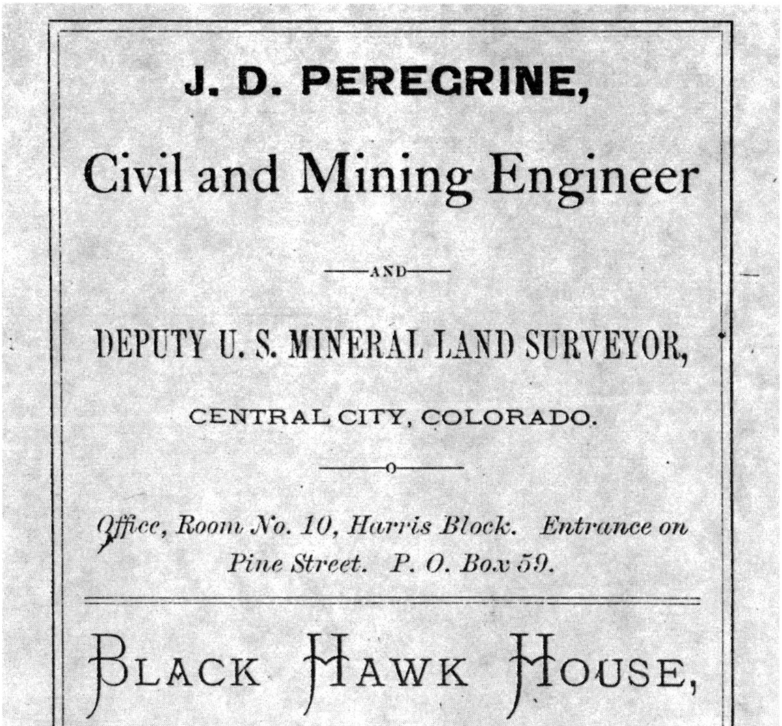

J. D. PEREGRINE,

Civil and Mining Engineer

——AND——

DEPUTY U. S. MINERAL LAND SURVEYOR,

CENTRAL CITY, COLORADO.

——o——

Office, Room No. 10, Harris Block. Entrance on Pine Street. P. O. Box 59.

BLACK HAWK HOUSE,

J. F. TABER, PROP.

THE ONLY FIRST-CLASS HOUSE IN THE CITY.

Livery Stable connected with the House.

EXCURSION PARTIES CAN BE ACCOMMO-DATED BY TELEGRAPHING.

EVERYTHING FIRST-CLASS

48

Collection of Freda and Francis B. Rizzari

Here are two advertisements from an early directory. At Black Hawk, J.F. Tabor operated a fine hostelry and stable.

Jake Sandelowski is the man wearing a vest but no hat. Harvey Doe appears at the right of the white door. The Sandelowski and Pelton Store stood in Black Hawk.

south of Gregory Gulch. Soon there were placer claims, water wheels, and sluice boxes in Leavenworth, Illinois, and other surrounding gulches.

Well before the first snows arrived there were already some 1,000 eager gold hunters at the sites. There were reports that gold production averaged about $35,000 each week. By the summer of 1860 there were approximately 2,500 people there. To protect themselves and the validity of their claims, they set up the Russell District, with rules patterned after those over the hill in Central City. Some of the Russell District's rules were quite liberal. For instance, only children under ten years of age could not hold claims. Also, all ladies in the Russell district had the same political rights as men.

Collection of Evelyn and Robert L. Brown

The late Guy Herstrom executed this fine pen and ink drawing of the Methodist Church at Russell Gulch, now gone.

Green Russell's duplex cabin (see chapter three)
was the first structure to appear in the new town.
Another of the earliest buildings was a school.
Fourteen students were enrolled as early as 1860.

Collection of Jim Wright

In Russell Gulch, the Barnabe and Ress Saloon was a very popular "watering place." It stood on the street below the Virginia Canyon Road.

Later a multi-storied school was built. Since Russell Gulch was always a family oriented place, there was also a pretty little Methodist Church standing just above the principal road, until it collapsed in the 1960s. A thriving business district flourished along a street parallel to the main road through town, where one could find the town hall, assorted "thirst quenchers," and a meat market. Most notable among

Collection of Nancy and Ed Bathke

This photograph by Joseph Collier, who had a Central City studio between 1872 and 1874, shows the destructive practice of hydraulic mining in Russell Gulch.

the drinking establishments was the Barnabe and Ress Saloon.

Although the placer claims lasted only four or five years, deep mining continued sporadically for another couple of decades. On the hillside above Russell

Gulch the superstructure of the Kemp Calhoun and Jefferson Calhoun Mines is still visible. These were the only pair of Gilpin County properties rich enough to justify sinking two adjacent shafts into the ground. By the early 1880s population had dwindled to a mere 400 persons. Some uranium was mined there as late as the 1920s, but not enough for another boom.

Green Russell left his town in 1862 and enlisted in a Confederate regiment formed back in his native Georgia. For some reason he was sent to serve in the Southwest. At one point he was arrested and subsequently released by Union troops stationed in Santa Fe. Following the battle at Appomattox he returned to Colorado, where he remained for about a decade. Then in 1875 Russell accompanied his Cherokee wife to Oklahoma's Indian Territory Reservation.

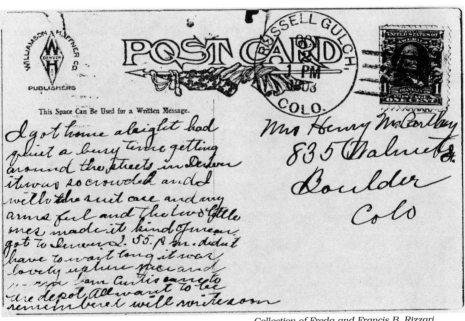

Collection of Freda and Francis B. Rizzari

This rare 1903 postcard carries the Russell Gulch postmark.

Collection of Jane and Louis Bass

In its heyday, Russell Gulch was spread along several streets. Its location is along the Virginia Canyon Road, southwest of Central City. In the background are the Indian Peaks.

Collection of Evelyn and Robert L. Brown

In this contemporary picture Russell Gulch is viewed from the identical place.

William G. Chamberlain's Denver Studio was in Denver between 1861 and 1881. He took this view of Chase Gulch, adjacent to Black Hawk.

During the prohibition era of the 1930s, Russell Gulch became a busy place once more as Denver bootleggers stashed their bathtub gin and illegal whiskey inside deserted mine shafts. One other story from this time persists and may or may not be true.

Collection of Mae Bertagnoli

This unique picture shows the community of American City. Notice the flag above the post office and the hotel with a turreted roof at right.

Collection of Evelyn and Robert L. Brown

In this contemporary view, most of the original structures are still visible.

Collection of Evelyn and Robert L. Brown

The town of Gilpin's location was northwest of Central City.
The background mountains are the Indian Peaks along the
Continental Divide.

from this time persists and may or may not be true.
Allegedly, the bootleggers themselves occasionally
went into hiding from lawmen inside the old mine
tunnels of Russell Gulch.

Today a few families still live in the town. I once
made the mistake of inquiring of an older resident,
"What do you people live off up here?" He was ready
for me and replied, "Each other."

In the autumn most of the trees in the surrounding meadows change to the usual gold, but there are
other groves around the old town that assume a bril-

liant orange hue, almost a red. It's worth a trip up to view them.

Three other towns, Apex, Nugget, and American City, were also neighbors of Central City and should also be regarded as "satellites." But all three were of a later vintage and did not exist in this earlier period. They date from the 1890s. Apex was a part of the Pine Creek Mining District.

At American City enough gold was found to warrant construction of a large mill, called the Mascot. American City's location is probably the most handsome of any of the Gilpin County towns. The snow-capped Continental Divide is clearly visible from the townsite. In 1911 the Selig-Polyscope Picture Company took advantage of it. They brought Tom Mix to the old town and filmed a couple of "oaters," the silent westerns that were so popular at the time. As noted in the following chapter, Mix's leading lady was Myrtle Steadman, whose brother was a Nevadaville saloon keeper.

Today almost nothing remains of Nugget. Apex still has a few original buildings, but a fire destroyed two of the best ones some years ago. Up on the hill at American City, several of the cabins have been restored for occupancy as summer homes. It easily qualifies as one of Colorado's best preserved semi-ghost towns.

Nearby there were two other towns named Wide Awake and Kingston. Kingston was a small place located on Pile Hill, on the trail between Nugget and Alice. The huge boardinghouse sported four gabled windows in the roof. It stood just below the multi-storied London Mine building. Unfortunately, it is gone now.

6.

NEVADAVILLE

ALTHOUGH NEVADAVILLE was also a satellite of Central
City, it was so unique and had such an unusual history that it deserves its own chapter. In common with
several of its neighbors, the town was born during the
summer of 1859. It was located in the broad valley
between Quartz and Gunnell Hills. In the beginning it
was known as the New Nevada of the Rocky
Mountains. At that time it was larger than Central
City, Black Hawk, or Denver City.

The rich Burrows Lode was found near Nevadaville, a scant three weeks after John Gregory's important find at Mountain City. Several of the best known
and richest mines, including the Ophir, Jones,
California, Hubert, Indiana, Casey, Hidden Treasure,
and the Kent County were located in Nevada Gulch.

Nevadaville had an identity problem unlike any
other Colorado town. For a while it was known as
Nevada City, but the postal service met with problems
when it tried to deliver the mails. Out in California
there was another town with the same name. Since
the abbreviations for California and Colorado were so
similar, the result was sometimes confusing in an era
when so many people were illiterate. Because

Collection of Fred and Jo Mazzulla

Before the fires, Nevadaville was photographed from the Quartz Hill mining road. Its post office was always known as Bald Mountain.

Collection of Evelyn and Robert L. Brown

From the Quartz Hill mining road, here is a contemporary picture of Nevadaville. A series of fires destroyed many of the original structures.

California's Nevada City was the oldest, it was given preference. The postal people dictated a name change for the Colorado town.

Nevadaville's post office had been established in January of 1861. Henceforth it was to be Bald Mountain, officially that is. But the residents disliked the name and refused to honor it. Even more, they disliked having the government meddling in their affairs. So the postal facility was always known as Bald Mountain, while the town refused to drop the Nevada City designation. Some years later, in 1868, Postmaster General Schuyler Colfax came to Nevada

Collection of Evelyn and Robert L. Brown

Here are several "short beer" saloon tokens and a dog tag from Nevadaville. The one at the upper left bears the Bald Mountain imprint.

City with an entourage of eastern dignitaries, hoping to finally put the controversy to rest. At that time Colfax was campaigning for the vice presidential nomination. Finally the impasse was bridged when both sides compromised on the name Nevadaville, but the post office was still known as Bald Mountain. This unpopular name is visible on one of the saloon "short beer" tokens in one of the photographs in this chapter.

In all of the history of Colorado there are only two or three instances of Indians attacking a town. For the most part this is the stuff of bad fiction and worse television. Native Americans were not stupid. Only a "Hollywood Indian" is that dumb. Nevertheless, there was an abiding fear in our frontier settlements that an Indian attack might occur. Nevadaville once experienced such a trauma. Whoever started this vicious rumor remains unknown, but the word spread quickly and sent whole families scurrying to the Odd Fellows Hall, the largest stone building in town. Some wives hurriedly baked cookies and made taffy, hoping to placate the warriors and send them away with full stomachs. The story was that a band of Utes was on the warpath and Nevadaville was their destination. Major J.M. Chivington's troops took to the trail and routed a band of Utes near Vasquez and Berthoud Passes. This ended the scare. Threats of Indian raids could nearly always be counted on to evoke panic. Too many people had read and believed the novels of James Fenimore Cooper. One day in Denver, the town drunk rode his mule out of the town a couple of miles, picked up a spent arrow and pushed it through his hat. He rode into town howling, "The Indians are coming!" Terrified citizens fled to a downtown stockade for safety. The drunk made the rounds of empty saloons, drinking for free. When another inebriate up in

Collection of Carolyn Bancroft

Among the pictures used in this book, this view of Nevadaville
is one of the earliest.

Collection of Evelyn and Robert L. Brown

Exposed in 1993, this view of Nevadaville matches the above
photograph.

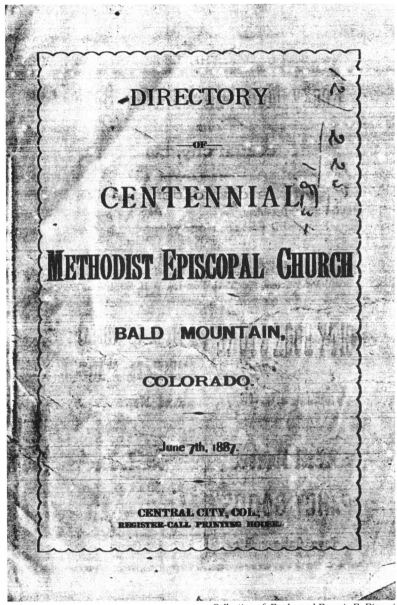

Here is the front page from the directory for the Methodist
Episcopal Church at Nevadaville. Note the 1887 date and use
of the Bald Mountain name.

Central City heard the good news, he tried the same trick. It worked for him, also.

In 1861, Nevadaville once again called attention to its population statistics. It had 2,705, while Denver's population was a scant 2,603. Its first government was not established until 1870. At that time a board of trustees was elected to run the town for one year. When the first election was held in 1878, D.H. Andrews was elected as the first mayor. Formal incorporation did not occur until July 7, 1870.

One of the district's first schools was established at Nevadaville. Since this was a family town, some 150 pupils attended classes that first year. The school building was a long, low, single level structure with four rooms. It was built on a centrally located hill to accommodate all sections of the town. Later the school's enrollment rose to 250. The staff consisted of a principal, who also taught classes, and three full-time teachers.

Nevadaville's Episcopal church was erected in 1860. By the turn of the century, population had dwindled to the point where the Episcopal pastor from Central City came up on Sunday evenings to conduct services. Originally, the Methodist church was connected with its sister institution over in Idaho Springs. The pastor was paid $700 each year. A frame structure housed the church until the building became inadequate. A brick building replaced it in 1894. At the turn of the century the church membership totaled forty persons, but for some reason their Sunday School classes attracted 150 young people each week.

For most of its years, a wide assortment of business establishments lined Nevadaville's Main Street, including thirteen saloons. Prominent among them was the Miner's Arms Saloon, owned by Thomas

Courtesy University of Colorado

This view looks northwest across Nevadaville. Both churches
are discernible at the far right.

Collection of Evelyn and Robert L. Brown

This view of Nevadaville was taken in August of 1974. Notice
the large mine dump at the same place in both pictures.

Chapple. Chapple first opened it in 1880. It continued to operate for more than three decades. Thomas H. Lawry operated the Bon Ton, a very popular name for a saloon at that time. Irish Mike Steadman called his thirst quencher the Silver Dollar. Mike's sister, Myrtle, was Tom Mix's leading lady in the silent films he made in Gilpin County, mostly at American City. Steve Jelbert's saloon tokens were octagonal in shape and were of the twelve-and-a-half cent short beer check variety. S.H. Grenfell chose the unpopular name of Bald Mountain Saloon for his place. An example of his token is in one of the accompanying photographs. Joseph and Matt Kramer arrived from Germany in 1868. A still extant document dated November 1, 1907, was printed on the letterhead of the town of Nevadaville. It gave Matt Kramer permission to operate a saloon for one year. A fee of $250 was to be paid twice yearly. The Kramer brothers first opened their doors in 1890. One of their great attractions was a pool table. John Maddern's Gold Coin Saloon was conceded to have been the most popular one in town, possibly because Maddern was a member of the town council.

Quite apart from all those drinking establishments, there were many other businesses along Nevadaville's Main Street. John C. Kloer arrived in town in 1898 and opened a barbershop in the Masonic Temple in 1908. A second tonsorial parlor, owned by John H. Fuhr, appeared in 1899. Thomas O. Davey started a shoe store in 1885. In spare moments he also did shoe and boot repairs. In 1892, a grocery store was opened by Cornishman Richard Rowling in the Odd Fellows Building. It was destroyed by a fire the following year. Undaunted, Rowling reopened in another location.

Courtesy University of Colorado

A large mine dump north of Nevadaville provided the vantage point for this photographer. The main thoroughfare runs horizontally across the bottom of the picture.

Collection of Evelyn and Robert L. Brown

In 1991, Evelyn and I climbed this prominence to record a view of Nevadaville. Notice that some original buildings still stand.

J.H. Nankervis, whose parents brought him to Nevadaville in 1877, when he was just seven years old, became the town's butcher. His shop was in the Red Men's Building, the largest structure in town. Nankervis specialized in beef, lamb, pork, and wild game in season. Curiously, the accepted medium of exchange was gold dust. Since there was never a bank in town, merchants commonly kept candy pails behind their counters for the dust.

Dr. C.A. Bourke came down from Canada in 1890 and set up a medical practice. He also had an apothecary shop that sold medicines, books, perfumes, and tobacco. Gents' furnishings, chinaware, lamps, utensils, tinware, oils, and grain could be purchased at

Collection of Evelyn and Robert L. Brown

Looking north across Nevadaville, the tracks are probably to one of the mines.

A GRAND

MUSICAL · AND · DRAMATIC

ENTERTAINMENT

WILL BE GIVEN

At Cannon's Hall

SATURDAY EVENING, APRIL 14, 1894

BY THE

Nevadaville Brass **BAND**

Composed of the following artists

N. H. GRENFELL, BANDMASTER.

Richard Grenfell.
Thomas Rowe.
James Bennetts.
Benjamin Waters.
Thomas Pope.

James Angwin.
Henry Grenfell.
Nicholas Grenfell.
Martin Williams.

And the Young People's Dramatic Association

FOR BENEFIT OF BRASS BAND.

THE FOLLOWING PROGRAM WILL BE PRESENTED.

OVERTURE - - - (Linwood) by Band

Domestic Drama in Two Acts,

The Chimney Corner

THE CAST:

Patty Probity - - - - - Janie Angwin

Collection of Freda and Francis B. Rizzari

In Nevadaville, Cannon's Hall was a popular place for both plays and band concerts, sometimes both in the same evening.

MUSICAL and DRAMATIC

ENTERTAINMENT.

AT CANNON'S HALL, NEVADAVILLE.

Friday Evening, August 17th, 1894.

—— GIVEN BY THE ——

✦ YOUNG PEOPLE'S ✦

DRAMATIC ASSOCIATION

— ASSISTED BY THE —

✻ NEVADAVILLE BRASS BAND ✻

The original Comedy-Drama, in four acts, entitled,

STRIFE

—— OR ——

MASTER and MEN.

—— CAST OF CHARACTERS: ——

Judge Buttons, retired judge and wealthy mill owner . . . Thos. Roberts

Collection of Freda and Francis Rizzari

Here is a Nevadaville playbill, badly faded, from 1894.

the Colorado Trading and Investment Company. There was never a dance hall in the town. There are still descendants of both the Grenfell and Nankervis families living in Golden.

The famous Newhouse Tunnel connected Nevada Gulch with Idaho Springs. The Kansas, one of the earliest mines, was worked through this tunnel. In 1876, a canal was completed to bring water across from Fall River to Nevadaville. It cost $60,000. Nevadaville had an active volunteer fire department that occupied the ground floor of the City Hall. Its membership was limited to forty men who used a chemical engine with a hose attachment and a hook and ladder pumper. Despite all of those saloons, a temperance society flourished, too. It was called the Independent Society of Good Templars.

In addition to the visit of Schuyler Colfax, a couple of other well-known persons also came to Nevadaville. Henry M. Stanley, the far-famed explorer of Africa, once came to town in search of material for his book on Colorado's gold mines. J. F. Tabor, brother of Senator H.A.W. "Silver Dollar" Tabor, was a resident of Nevadaville for a time.

Throughout its years, Nevadaville burned five times. Once it was burned nearly in its entirety. The conflagration began in a grove of trees above the town. Merchants' goods and liquor from the many saloons were hastily moved into mine tunnels to avoid destruction. About fifty homes were lost. The date was 1884. The last fire was in 1914. An 1860 ditch was fabricated to bring water over from Peck Gulch, seven miles away. Both it and the 1876 water diversion from Fall River were dry, as were the town's wells. A substantial part of the town went up in smoke.

One of the buildings spared in the 1884 fire was the Masonic Lodge. It was founded in 1859 as Nevada

Collection of Evelyn and Robert L. Brown

From the spine of Nevada Gulch, this picture looks across the town of Nevadaville. Both churches are visible at the left while the two story brick Masonic Lodge appears at far right.

Masonic Lodge #4. Chartered in 1861, it remains as one of Colorado's oldest. It is the second oldest chartered lodge in the state. The present building dates from the 1870s. Originally, Nevada Lodge #4 was #36 in Kansas Territory. Its charter was signed by the Rev. John M. Chivington, First Grand Master. Several times in recent years the lodge has held pancake breakfasts in the lodge hall as a fundraising effort to help defray the costs of restoring the interior rooms. Other fraternal orders that flourished in Nevadaville included the I.O.O.F. Lodge, Nevada #6, dating from 1869; and Knights of Pythias, Richmond Lodge #37 chartered on September 13, 1888. It had forty-six

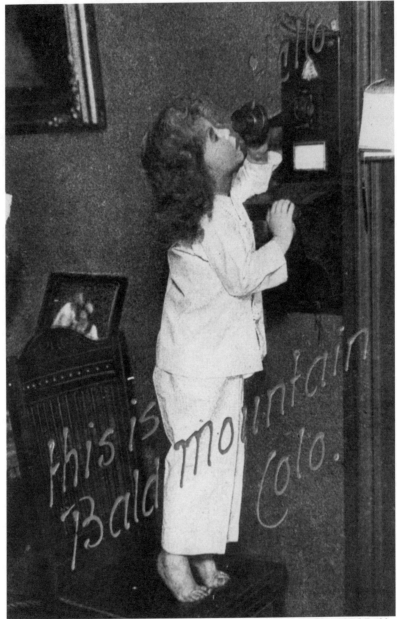

Collection of Nancy and Ed Bathke

This postcard carries the Bald Mountain logo. Bald Mountain
was the name of Nevadaville's post office.

members. The I.O.R.M. Lodge, Rising Sun Tribe #2 was organized in 1880 with ninety-seven members. The Daughters of Pocahontas, Osceola Council #5, was a ladies' auxiliary of the Red Men's Lodge. It had forty members when it was formed in 1894. The Knights of the Golden Eagle, Star of the West #3 was started in 1888. Its Silver Star Auxiliary was begun in 1899.

In the 1890 census, Nevadaville's population count had dwindled to a scant 1,200. The exodus out of the town began in 1878–9, when carbonate of lead bearing silver was found at Leadville. Many former gold miners from Nevadaville packed up and moved over to Lake County. One account suggests that close to half of the population of Nevada Gulch made the move. When silver was demonitized in 1893, the result was a panic and a mild recession. For whatever reason, the Gilpin County miners chose not to return to their former homes. One possible reason could have been the even richer deposits of gold that had just been found in the Cripple Creek District. Movement from one booming district to another was a common phenomenon in mining frontiers all across the American West.

Despite occasional Irish–Cornish rowdiness, Nevadaville was a family type town during most of its years. In its earliest days the population was predominantly male, and they soon tired of doing their own laundry and cooking their own stomach abusing meals. Soon there was help. Several widows arrived in town to open hotels and boardinghouses. These were profitable enterprises. The widows had been attracted by Nevadaville's reputation as a safe place to raise their children. After all, schools and churches already existed, and those were good barometers of a town's climate. Nevadaville's young ladies were counseled to

Public ◆ School
◆ENTERTAINMENT,◆
Bald Mountain, June 23, '96.

PROGRAMME.

PART I.

Graduating Exercises Eighth Grade.

Class Prophecy..Edith Noble
Address to Class...Maud Richards
Recitation—Lincoln's Last Dream........ ....Marie Nankervis
Presentation of Diplomas......................................Pres. Stevens
Farewell Address..Principal Snyder

PART II.

Piano Solo..Georgia Richards
Chorus—Famous Welch March...............................School
Ring Drill, by.........Agnes Sennett, Essie Trezise, Rose Richards,
    Mary Walls, Mamie Whitman, Mamie Mayhew, Edna Tuck,
    Ethel Bolitho, March Belcher, Mary Dennis, Julia Henry, Sadie
    Luty.
"A perfect body makes a chariot in which a heroic soul may well be
  proud to ride."   Henry Ward Beecher.
Recitation—Seein' things at night...................Richard Trezise
Song of the Flowers...:..........:.................Primary Children
Postures, "The body is not an end in itself, but must be trained to
  be the able and obedient servant of the mind; then it becomes a
  thing of power and dignity."—W. W. Parsons.
               1. Expectation, attention—backward, pity.
2. Determination, Fear, Renewed courage. 3. Exultation, Relig-
ious devotion. 4. Thought, Rejection, Resignation, Vindication.
5. Guarding against danger, Pleading Mercury—pose. 6. Modesty,
Supplication, Admiration. By Agnes Sennett, Marie Nankervis,
Minnie Feeley, Maud Richards, Susie Lawry, Katie Kramer, Maud
Prouse, Georgia Richards.
Song—Hunting We Will Go..............Intermediate Department

PART III.

OPERETTA.

TOO = BAD

Or Discontented Judith.

CAST OF CHARACTERS.

Judith (Soprano).......................................Edith Trezise.
Nurse   "   ....Maud Richards.
Betsy (Mezzo-Soprano)...........................Agnes Sennett
Mother   "   ....Marie Nankervis
Old Woman or Fairy (Mezzo-Soprano)..............Edith Noble.

Wagoners, Haymakers, Labourers, Milkmaids, School Children.

ARGUMENT.

Judith, a little girl living in a comfortable home, is discontented and peevish.
She has a habit of saying that everything is "too bad." Her nurse remonstrates
with her in vain. Betsy, a little girl who is being brought up to poverty and hard
work in a cottage, appears upon the scene, and Judith wishes she could live
Betsy's life. An old woman in a red cloak, who is a fairy in disguise, accosts
Judith, and after a conversation gives her an apple which she has only to bite be-

Collection of Freda and Francis Rizzari

Although this playbill from the Nevadaville school dates from
1896, it still carries the early Bald Mountain name.

Courtesy Denver Public Library, Western History Collection

From the base of Quartz Hill, this clear photograph shows Nevadaville in a happier time. Most buildings were constructed on Cornish stone foundations, many of which still exist.

avoid men with manicured fingernails. Unless a man's hands showed signs of toil, he was probably untrustworthy, a gambler, or both and should be shunned. Nevadaville was that kind of town. Incidentally, at one time a small community called Dogtown existed along the road between Nevadaville and Central City.

Today the original City Hall, with its jail and fire department, still stands. Across the street is the Masonic Lodge. Next to the lodge, the old Joseph and Matt Kramer Saloon building now contains a book store that specializes in Western Americana. Some homes and several mines are still in existence.

Despite its proximity to several metropolitan areas, Nevadaville has somehow been spared the vandalism that plagues many of Colorado's abandoned mining towns. Early in 1991, television discovered Gilpin County. Several scenes for one of the Perry Mason shows, "The Case of the Glass Coffin," were taped in both Central City and Nevadaville. The Nevadaville episode involved one of the old mines and an automobile chase down the dusty length of Main Street. Nevadaville's picturesque location and still standing original structures make it worth seeing.

7.

THE IRISH AND CORNISH

FOLLOWING CLOSELY on the heels of the Anglo–Americans, three different ethnic groups appeared in Gilpin County. The Irish were the first on the scene. Next came the Cornish, who probably were among the world's ablest miners and stone masons. Last of the ethnic people to appear were the hard-working Chinese, who fanned out across the American West following the completion of the Central Pacific portion of the transcontinental railroad. The Chinese contributions appear in the following chapter.

Europe's Industrial Revolution had a number of unfortunate aspects, leaving many workers unemployed because of the introduction of labor-saving machinery. Since most of Europe offered no haven for displaced persons, many looked to the United States, in particular to our frontier, as a place for both skilled and unskilled workmen, especially the Irish, who were in search of new homes. Unlike the Scots–Irish who had come earlier from the north of Ireland, these new immigrants were Celtic Roman Catholics from Ireland's southern counties.

Overpopulation, political opposition, religious persecution, along with the failure of the potato crop in 1845 hastened their departure for America. Upon their arrival in the cities along the Atlantic seaboard, their numbers swelled the population to the point where job-seekers in Boston, for example, found any number of "Irish must not apply" signs in windows of business establishments. To escape low paying jobs and life in the squalid shanty towns of eastern cities, many Irish headed into the West.

Being somewhat clannish, the Irish judiciously avoided the slave-holding South, viewing it as being too much like the absentee landlordism they had migrated to escape. During the Civil War, the Union Army persuaded large numbers of Irish to enlist as a means of getting a fresh start in their new homeland. Following conclusion of the conflict, additional Irish fled, entering the West to seek a wider and deeper rut. They also sought to escape the growing profusion of Pat and Mike stories that were typical of the growing anti–Irish prejudice. Fairly large numbers came to Colorado to seek unskilled work in the mines. Nearly half of Nevadaville's population was of Irish extraction

The Irish were adventurous, fun-loving, energetic, superstitious, and inclined to associate mostly with other Irishmen. Tom Walsh was one such Irishman who lived in Nevadaville for a time. Later he migrated to Colorado's San Juan Mountains after the discovery of gold and silver in the region. His fabulous Camp Bird Mine above Ouray brought him both fame and a vast fortune.

Patrick D. Casey was typical of Nevadaville's "Shanty Irish." He apparently had landed in New York sometime in the mid–1850s, illiterate and without funds. Two difficult years as a day laborer followed. Discouraged, he crossed the Great Plains to Colorado Territory in 1859. Arriving in Nevadaville he staked out a 100-foot-long claim on the Burroughs Lode, rolled up his sleeves, and went to work.

Pat's log cabin stood on the south side of Nevada Gulch. He was a character in the most appealing sense of the word. His inability to read or write, plus a love of liquor, have led to the profusion of Pat Casey stories repeated with much gusto in Gilpin County, even today. Perhaps ten percent have any validity. Most of them have been embellished with each retelling. Mark Twain once observed that, "Many stirring events in history happened to the wrong people in the wrong place and at the wrong time. The conscientious historian will remedy these defects." And so it probably was with Pat Casey.

Following many months of hard labor, cave-ins, and poor assays, Pat Casey's mine on Quartz Hill became a rich producer, probably in April or May of 1862. He bought land in Chase Gulch and had a thirty-two-stamp mill erected to refine his ores. With wealth came notoriety and humorous tales about the Irishman. To properly appreciate a telling of the Casey yarns, a person capable of feigning a music hall Irish accent is preferred. If the teller can partly close one eye while cocking his head to one side, so much the better. The following are a few of my own favorites.

Having endured so much personal hardship during the lean years, Pat felt genuine compassion for the crews of men working underground in his Casey Mine. His compassion was particularly evident after several drinks. Pat would drive his horse-drawn buggy close to the mine opening. While leaning over the open hole he would yell down the shaft, "How many of yese [sic] is there down there tonight?"

Usually it would be an odd number, but Casey had never mastered subtraction. If the answer was "seven" or "nine" or some such total, Pat would yell

Courtesy State Historical Society of Colorado Library

This view of Nevadaville looks northwest across the town. Before the fires, Nevadaville was larger than Denver. The horse drawn wagon in the lower foreground was on the Quartz Hill road leading to Pat Casey's mine.

again, "Well, half of yese come up and the rest stay down."

Pat would take those who came to the top to a saloon and treat them to several rounds of drinks before returning them to the mine. Then Casey brought the remaining workers to the surface and treated them to libations before returning to his cabin for the night. His horse always knew the way home if the master was too intoxicated to handle the reins.

Another of the Casey fables describes how Mary York Cozens met Pat on the street one day while soliciting funds to build a Catholic church for Father

Machebeuf. She reminded Pat of his Irish–Catholic heritage and asked for fifty dollars toward construction of the house of worship. Because he was ignorant about money denominations, Pat sometimes kept a mathematically astute youngster at his side. On this occasion he instructed the boy to give Mrs. Cozens the requested sum. Mary looked covetously at the still remaining bulk of his pouch and commented, "You know, Mr. Casey, if ye was to give us another fifty dollars we could buy a fine new chandelier for the church."

Casey thought for a moment before replying, "Sure, and take another fifty dollars, but I don't know who in the hell you'll ever get to play the thing."

Pat's work crew from the mine was known throughout the Central City environs as "Pat Casey's Night Hands." Their drinking and carousing bouts were almost legendary. Mike Dougherty and his traveling theatrical company often played at Central City's Montana Theatre. Dougherty decided to write an operetta called Pat Casey's Night Hands. It played successfully in Denver on several occasions. When Pat heard about it, he threatened to bring the Night Hands down from Nevadaville to wreck the theater and the city if the offensive operetta was ever staged in Central City. Dougherty accepted the challenge and booked his show into the Montana Theatre.

On the appointed evening, Casey and his crew came down the hill. They made several rounds of the saloons, uttering dark threats. By curtain time most of them had passed out in the aisles. The show went on and was an artistic triumph. Sheriff Billy Cozens helped Casey and his men leave town, somewhat to the chagrin of the residents who had looked forward to observing a donnybrook. Unfortunately, the show's score has not survived.

My own favorite among the Pat Casey stories involves how he got around his Irish–Catholic convictions on Fridays. At a time when Roman Catholics were admonished to eat fish on Fridays, Pat had a weekly problem with his conscience. It seems that he intensely disliked seafood. So on Fridays, he would enter Nevadaville's meat market, approach the proprietor and inquire, "And would ye be havin' any whale?"

To which the owner would reply, "No, Mr. Casey, no whale today."

Then Pat would cock his head and say, "Then give me two pork chops, and the Lord knows I've asked for fish."

Pat Casey owned a fine watch, but was unable to tell time. So when someone would ask him what time it was, Pat would pull the watch out and say, "See fer yerself sos you'll know I'll not be lyin' to yez."

A few years later, flush with money from the Casey Mine, Pat went to New York City to see the sights. His hotel had so many floors that he felt obliged to blaze a trail in the woodwork with a hatchet in order to find his room again when returning from evening sojourns around the city. It cost him $2,000 for repairs. Upon his arrival back in Nevadaville, he announced, "Me name's no longer Pat, but P.D. Casey, Isquire [sic]."

A few years later, he embarked upon a second pilgrimage to New York, played the stock market and made a number of unwise investments. Predictably, he dissipated most of his fortune in about ten riotous years and never located a second bonanza. When last heard from, he was just one of the down-and-out prospectors in the Black Hills rush to South Dakota in 1876. No photograph of Casey exists, but there is one of his cabin.

Because of the prejudice that had followed the Irish westward, Central City once tried to discourage their presence in town after sundown. It was widely believed that Irishmen ate peas with their knives and enjoyed beating their wives regularly on Saturday nights. Most of the Irish were more comfortable living up in Nevadaville. A casual perusal of state business directories reveals a preponderance of Irish names. But even in Nevadaville, there were misunderstandings, primarily with the Cornish. Possibly as a result, most Irish families lived in just one part of the town. In part, the Irish–Cornish feuds were based on religious Catholic–Protestant differences and economic competition. In Nevadaville, there were only two churches. One was Methodist and the other was Episcopalian. The Irish, being Catholic, journeyed down the hill to attend services in Central City.

Living apart was of no assistance in resolving these animosities. Each weekend their quarrels erupted in fist fights, broken bones, and sometimes shootings. Most of the bloody encounters happened in Nevadaville, but sometimes they boiled over into Central City. But when Italian and Austrian miners appeared in the late 1880s, the long-standing quarrels subsided and both the Irish and Cornish united against the new arrivals. Down in Central City, the wife of Dr. Robert A'Duddell remembered weekends spent busily threading needles for her husband, as he sewed together the cracked skulls of pugilists who came staggering down the hill from Nevadaville. Her husband was once called to repair five heads damaged in a saloon brawl, where bar stools had been used as weapons. At times, the donnybrooks resulted in fatalities, but charges of murder were rarely filed. It was impossible to determine who had done what, with which, and to whom. In general, both the Irish and

the Cornish preferred to settle matters among themselves rather than having their quarrels publicly aired
in the outsiders' Anglo–American courts.

In almost equal isolation, the Cornish lived at the
opposite end of the community. Although precise
dates are difficult to document, the Cornish left the
lead mines of Wisconsin and the copper pits of
Michigan, and probably began to arrive in Colorado
during the spring of 1862. At home in Cornwall, they
had gained centuries of mining experience laboring in
the tin mines. It was the Cornish who first introduced
the system of contract mining to America. Richard
Pearce, a Cornishman, introduced a smelting process
that revolutionized Colorado's complex quartz mining,
recovering over seventy-five percent of the gold.
Pearce is also credited with discovering pitchblende
(uranium) in North America. He was taking a hike
near Russell Gulch at the time. Although he was born
in Pennsylvania, the mining baron–philanthropist
Spencer Penrose was a Cornishman. Penrose made a
fortune in Arizona copper, Cripple Creek gold, and
built both the Broadmoor Hotel and the automobile
road up Pikes Peak. Incidentally, in Gilbert and
Sullivan's ever popular operetta, *The Pirates of
Penzance,* the fictional buccaneers were Cornishmen.
King Arthur's legendary Camelot is thought to have
been in Cornwall.

The guttural, throaty speech of the Cornish con-
founded most Americans. They spoke a quaint and
almost unintelligible Celtic tongue, somewhat akin to
the Welsh language. Among other things, they con-
stantly misplaced the letter *h* when speaking. Sometimes it was added, and at other times it was simply
misplaced. They included the *h* at the beginning of
words that had no *h* and deleted the *h* where it should
have been. Thus an English characteristic that was

adopted naturally by the Cornish people resulted in a unique manner of speaking.

People from Cornwall also had a habit of calling persons to whom they spoke by such endearing terms as "my son," "my 'andsome," or "my beauty." Additionally, they frequently added the word *you* after a statement. If one inquired for a Cousin Jack's health, the reply might be, "Some grand you." Gender was commonly ascribed to inanimate objects. Cornish men and women substituted the words *thee* and *thou* in place of *you.*

Cornish miners often contracted miner's consumption, actually silicosis, from working underground. Under such conditions, the lungs are filled with rock dust until breathing becomes difficult. As a consequence, any strenuous exertion became impossible and miners were forced to quit work at age thirty or thirty-five. Lacking welfare or family assistance programs, Cornish women tried to provide for their family's livelihood by taking in laundry, scrubbing floors, running a boarding house, or doing domestic work in other people's homes.

In Gilpin County, Cornishmen were soon nicknamed Cousin Jacks, since whenever someone had a job to be filled, the Cornish nearly always claimed to have a cousin named Jack back in Cornwall who would gladly come over and take the job, if a ticket to America would become available. Their wives were called Cousin Jennies. The hard working Cornish accepted the terms with good humor.

Yuletide customs and traditions of the Cornish, as with other ethnic groups, had been brought over from their homeland. On Christmas Eve, they carried bushes consisting of two interlocking decorated evergreen circles with lighted candles at the base of the hoops. They walked from mine to mine while singing

Western History Department, Denver Public Library

In this picture the tiny Gilpin Tram engine is bringing four loaded ore cars downgrade in Chase Gulch toward the refining mills at Black Hawk.

From the collection of Evelyn and Robert L. Brown

In this contemporary view we see the same built-up Cornish wall and the identical hills of Chase Gulch.

their rare and haunting native carols. Each Cornish household displayed a wassail bowl filled with native libations served with saffron cakes to guests. Their pasties, small meat and vegetable pies, are still popular. Cornish Jennies often served pasties to the families in homes where they worked as domestics.

May Day was also special to the Cousin Jacks. May baskets filled with delicacies were left on doorsteps of popular boys and girls. Following a rap on the door, the recipient of the basket was expected to pursue the donor, rewarding him or her with a chaste hug and a kiss. Spirited wrestling bouts were likewise popular among the Cornish. Drilling contests were held regularly.

Both the Cornish and Central City folks spent many weekends observing these lively contests. One of the most entertaining contributions of the Cornish was their belief that all deep mines were peopled by tiny gnomes, only a couple of feet tall. They were know as Tommy Knockers, and they made thumping sounds to warn miners of an impending cave-in. Superstitious Cousin Jacks would instantly leave any mine when they heard such sounds. They also held tenaciously to the belief that the presence of a woman underground meant bad luck. As recently as the construction of the Eisenhower Tunnel, men walked off the job when female engineers were hired to work alongside them.

Cornish as well as Irish humor was popular among many segments of the Gilpin County population. Much of it was ribald and dealt with the somewhat casual sexual attitudes among the Cousin Jacks and Jennies. Such stories were repeated with high good humor by the non–Cornish. A few examples of the less offensive yarns follow:

When a Cousin Jack observed a stuffed owl in the window of a Central City shop, he promptly asked the owner, "'Ow much do thee want for that broad faced chicken?"

"That's no chicken," replied the store man, "that's an owl!"

"Damme [sic]," replied the Jack, "I dusen't [sic] care 'ow auld it is, what do thee want for it?"

In common with the Irish, many Cornishmen were illiterate. On one occasion, a Cousin Jack looked at a newspaper picture of a train and observed, "Damme, some bloody wreck 'ere." He was holding the newspaper upside down at the time.

On another occasion, a Jack once held out his closed hand to a young schoolboy in Nevadaville. "Look 'ere, sonny, if thee can tell me 'ow many pennies in me 'and, thee can 'ave all five of 'em."

"Five," replied the boy.

"Damme, take 'em all, thee'rt a genius," replied the Cornishman.

When a Jack wanted to send a letter to his intended back in Cornwall, he dictated it to a literate friend. Then he insisted that the writer must read it back to him. But first, he placed his own hands over the other man's ears to preclude his hearing the written endearments.

Both the Irishman and the Cornishman, each in his own way, were unique. When both groups lived and worked in the same region, as they did in Gilpin County, life sometimes became interesting and occasionally difficult. Descendants of both groups were readily assimilated into Colorado's body politic. Even today, numbers of their offspring still reside in Gilpin County and in Golden. With time, their once fierce differences have been lost in the mists of yesterday.

8.

THE CHINESE ARRIVE

SOME YEARS AFTER THE IRISH, CORNISH, and southern Europeans came to Gilpin County, the Chinese arrived. It was the 1849 gold rush to California that first lured large numbers of the Celestials to America. Nearly all of them were hard workers who paid scant attention to the prevailing twelve hour work day, preferring to labor from dawn to dusk, and for most modest wages. In the beginning, most of them had planned to save their pay for a return to China, where the pittances they had earned assured them an opulent lifestyle.

A second element that made the Chinese desirable additions to anyone's work crew was their steadfast refusal to join unions or to strike. As the mining frontier spread eastward out of California the demand for low-priced laborers led to the growth of Chinese settlements in Nevada, Idaho, Montana, Arizona, and elsewhere.

Then, as mining frontiers collapsed or went into periodic slumps, the Chinese sought other employment. As this was also the time of Western railroad building and expansion, substantial numbers of Chinese switched over to work for a variety of the

Western lines, principally as track layers. It was the Irish who put down the tracks and ties of the eastern part of the Transcontinental Railroad. The Chinese were the laborers on the Central Pacific or western end. They were paid ten cents a day. When the two lines joined in Utah on May 10, 1869, the Chinese were out of work and soon migrated to other states, including Colorado. Once arrived, they hoped to mine and to build other railroads.

Colorado's first Chinese came down from Wyoming during the summer of 1870. For a time they worked on the Denver Pacific Railroad, a branch line of the Union Pacific that was build south from Cheyenne to the Territorial Capital in Denver. Georgetown donated a silver spike. On the initial run it took five hours to traverse the 100 or so miles from Cheyenne to Denver, although they ran the trains on a schedule fifty-five minutes ahead of Denver time. A second railroad, the Kansas Pacific, also employed Chinese workers. It entered Denver from the east later that year, 1870. James Archer of the Kansas Pacific demanded a two million dollar bribe to run the line into Denver. On the first runs, they carried dogs on the front of each train to scare the wild Texas cattle off the tracks, a practice the fun-loving Chinese found to be hilarious.

In 1869, William A.H. Loveland planned his Colorado Central Railroad, soon to be built up Clear Creek Canyon from Golden into Gilpin County. The Chinese would help to build it, too. These workers sent most of their pay to their families back in China, where it did nothing to help the economy of Gilpin County: a circumstance met with bitter resentment by the Anglo majority as well as the business community.

Chinese laborers worked long hours to complete the final four miles of narrow gauge track from Black Hawk up to Central City. Upon its completion, the Chinese stayed on. Many of them hired out as day laborers in the mines. Over 100 of them lived in a poverty-ridden section, known as Cameron's Camp, named for Alex Cameron, their employer. An even dozen of them lived huddled together in each tiny shack. George Crofutt, author of the widely popular *Grip-Sack Guide of Colorado*, observed a group of Chinese living in the abandoned Whipple and Excelsior Mills near Black Hawk. Later, they took over an abandoned section house in Cottonwood Gulch.

Mining was a better paying line of work than railroading and the industrious Chinese, wielding their tiny picks, worked in many Central City mines. Inevitably, in spare moments they did laundry. Soon there were a dozen or so Chinese prostitutes doing "horizontal work" in Central City and Black Hawk brothels. The late Louis Carter, an able Central City historian, once described how young children made "tick-tacks" from empty thread spools, a piece of copper wire, and a length of string. They notched the raised edges of the spools, inserted the wire through the hole, and wrapped the cord around the spool. At night, the spools would be placed against the window glass as the thread was given a fast pull. When placed against the window of a Chinese home, the fun began. The noise inside was startling, and usually brought one or more of the Celestials outside to chase the boys. Since the Chinese "talked funny," the boys' merriment was complete.

Perhaps it was because they looked different, maybe it was the sing-song quality in their speech that lent itself to mimicry by the children. Whatever it was, the Chinese were the subject of far more dis-

Collection of Sue and George Godfrey

After the railroad was completed, quite a few Chinese people moved down to Denver. Central Presbyterian Church was one of the denominations that sympathized with their plight. This group was photographed on the church steps in 1896.

crimination than the Irish or Cornish people. Few parents ever disciplined their progeny for "ragging the Chinks."

Two fires, in 1873 and again in 1874, swept Central City. The second one provoked a profound anti–Chinese sentiment in the town. The late Muriel Sibell Wolle once told this writer that nearly all Colorado mining towns burned at least once. Georgetown had a crack fire department and was spared. Somehow, Black Hawk never had a big fire either. Many of its 1860s buildings are still in use. Rosita burned three times, Nevadaville had five fires, and Central City had two.

The first conflagration, in 1873, did not destroy the entire town. It was a night fire that wiped out about sixteen buildings on Lawrence Street. A malfunctioning flue in Saint Paul's Church was the culprit. A blaze erupted and spread to the roof. Suddenly, a brisk wind came up and the fire jumped to other nearby buildings. Some buildings were blown up to create fire breaks. Despite the efforts of a hastily formed bucket brigade, it lasted most of the night.

When the fire that erupted in May of 1874 swept the town, results were far more serious. Consequently, the year 1874 is even now recalled as the year of the great fire. Unfortunately for the Chinese, the fire's source was one of their opium dens or laundries, located within the Oriental ghetto on lower Spring Street. It was a highly combustible shack, covered with tar paper. The locals called it a washie-washie house. During a religious observance, ceremonial joss sticks were placed on top of a bed of live coals. Another brisk breeze, as in 1873, complicated things.

The coals suddenly flamed up. The ensuing fire got out of hand and the laundry structure quickly became a raging inferno. The wind carried sparks to other Spring Street structures. Three thoroughly frightened laundry men came running from the burning shack. Central City's fire bell sounded its doleful alarm. The usual bucket brigade was hurriedly assembled, but the supply of gulch water had dried up.

Owners of nearby homes hurriedly piled their personal belongings in the streets by their houses.

Huge stacks of household goods, as well as merchandise from stores and shops, were carried to what they hoped would be places of safety. Money and securities from the bank were stuffed into lard cans for safekeeping.

In less than ten minutes, the fire had spread from Spring Street over to Eureka Street. As the blaze moved systematically up the street, Central City's firemen fought it there in the business district for a full three hours. Quite a few homes were knocked down and deliberately pushed into the flames to halt its spread. Two wells still contained water and were pressed into service.

Gradually, the fire died down of its own accord, primarily because so few burnable structures were still standing. Stone buildings and a few of the brick and masonry stores on Main Street were still there, although the fire gutted their interiors. In all, about 150 buildings, valued at half a million dollars, were gone. Golden loaded its fire engine onto a Colorado Central flatcar. It was able to reach Black Hawk, but there was no water available for the boiler and no mules to haul it up the hill into the midst of the raging inferno.

After the last hot spots of the fire had been extinguished, an angry mob located and cornered the unfortunate Chinese who had occupied the laundry shack where the blaze had started. They called the men "slant eyes," and a variety of other unprintable, disparaging epithets. Many in the crowd suggested loudly that because they were engaging in heathen practices, these men were to blame for the Central City fire. Leaders of the disorderly element accused the Orientals of everything except mainlining soy sauce. The Chinese were severely beaten, until more moderate persons intervened, rescued the hapless

Collection of Nancy and Ed Bathke

This rare Joseph Collier picture was taken the morning after Central City's "Great Fire of 1874." A pall of smoke still blankets the rubble as a man on horseback and other townspeople survey the damage.

captives, and spirited them away under cover of dark-ness. To assure their personal safety, they were hus-tled over to Georgetown.

For a time there was an effort to legislate the expulsion of all Chinese from Central City. Such a law was once passed over in Leadville. A Chinese Exclusion Act was passed in California, and our national Congress followed along by passing an Oriental Exclusion Act in 1882, 1892, and in 1902. Repeal did not come until 1943.

There was an extensive cleanup effort in the weeks following the fire. A relief committee arranged shelter for the homeless who had spent some chilly nights camped out on Gunnell Hill. In a surprisingly short time, most of the burned out area was rebuilt with new homes and business structures. Most of them are still there today. When the rich South Park placers gave out, many Chinese moved in. They paid the owners one dollar a head—and no one ever knew how much they took out.

In common with the Cornish and Irish, the Chinese have been assimilated into the mainstream of American life. Many of them are direct descendants of those who came to mine and to build railroads. They pay their taxes and their names rarely appear on wel-fare rolls. Their crime rate is next to nothing, one of our nation's lowest. Despite a rocky beginning, they have become good citizens, but at this writing none have elected to live in Central City.

9.

THE COLORADO CENTRAL RAIL-ROAD AND THE GILPIN TRAM

THE STORY OF A RAILROAD TO CONNECT Denver and Golden with Central City begins with the Colorado and Clear Creek Railroad, incorporated in February of 1865. It had hoped to build up through Clear Creek Canyon, from Golden to the mining camps of Gilpin County. In January of 1866, the company's name was changed to the Colorado Central and Pacific Railroad Company. Then in January of 1869, it changed again to become the Colorado Central Rail Road Company. This was the line destined to provide the anxiously awaited connection into Central City.

Competition between Denver and Golden was intense during these early years. After all, Golden had been the Territorial Capital prior to Denver. The Second Territorial Legislature had moved the first seat of government out of tiny Colorado City in 1862. Golden was Colorado Territory's second capitol until a popular vote in 1867, which transferred the honor to Denver.

William A.H. Loveland was the founder and leading citizen of Golden. He had hoped that someday,

Collection of Frances and Richard Ronzio

This Colorado Central excursion train on its way to Central City and Black Hawk paused at the Roscoe Placer. Always a popular stop, the riders often exited the cars to pose with the locomotive.

somehow, his town would surpass Denver. Loveland had labored earnestly to block completion of the Denver Pacific by constructing a division line north from Golden to a point known as Jersey. Curiously, the location of Jersey has never been authenticated. If successful, this would channel the railroad's business away from Denver in favor of his beloved Golden. Loveland and his partners, Edward L. Berthoud and Henry Teller, had raised $100,000 in bonds to finance a rail connection into Golden. With encouragement and assistance from the giant Union Pacific, construction of the Colorado Central began in May of 1868.

Collection of Nancy and Ed Bathke

During construction days this Colorado Central locomotive hauled ties to the workers near Packard Gulch. Central City is visible in the background.

Collection of Evelyn and Robert L. Brown

In this view many things of historic interest are obscured by trees that grew back on the hillside. The old Teller House Hotel, now a casino, is visible in both pictures.

Collection of Nancy and Ed Bathke

This grade was to have been a part of the new Central City Railroad, connecting it with the Moffat Line. It was never constructed.

Despite the bonds, other financial support was inadequate and progress was slow. For one thing, Loveland paid mightily to obtain that right-of-way from Golden to Jersey. This stretch of track was not finished until September 24, 1870. Although Loveland had expected Golden to be the principal beneficiary of his railroad, it was not working out that way.

In the interim, Loveland and Henry Teller approached the stalled Kansas Pacific, hoping to convince them that they should lay their standard gauge tracks to Jersey and complete the connection with Golden. But Governor John Evans, David Moffat, and their Denver backers shifted their work crews of "gandy dancers" from the already completed Denver Pacific to finally finish the Kansas Pacific line into Denver. Pine ties were floated down the South Platte River to Denver. Construction began east from Denver, hoping to intersect the Kansas Pacific.

The two lines met some forty miles east of the city and Loveland was frustrated again. In just two months after the arrival of the Denver Pacific, the first Kansas Pacific locomotive rolled in on August 15, 1870. Now Denver had two railroads and Golden still had none.

In the spring of 1861, Loveland and F.J. Ebert made the initial railroad survey in Colorado Territory. One part called for a projected line up the canyon from Golden to Black Hawk. Almost at once Loveland's survey crews were busy laying the groundwork and plotting the grades. Instead of the usual standard gauge, this one was to be a three foot wide narrow gauge, ideally suited for turning the canyon's tight corners. It was the Colorado Central's chief engineer, Edward Berthoud, who first considered abandoning the standard gauge line that the original sur-

No. 8 - SNOWY RANGE

Collection of Nancy and Ed Bathke

This Weitfle picture, called "Snowy Range," was taken on the line between Central City and Black Hawk.

Collection of Nancy and Ed Bathke

"Snowy Range Passenger Car" was Charles Weitfle's name for
this view on the Colorado Central line to Central City.

vey had stipulated. Berthoud examined the tortuous, twisting defile above Golden and finally was able to convince Loveland that a narrow gauge made more sense. Besides, the smaller railroad would be less expensive to construct, notwithstanding the costs of tunnels and bridges that would be necessary.

Incidentally, Loveland had dreamed of extending his line westward, too, if he could locate a low enough pass through the mountains. Engineer Berthoud retained the capable but eccentric Jim Bridger to assist in the search. Bridger was one of those rare persons who could adapt to harsh living conditions during the dangerous fur trade period, and lived to tell about it. Nobody knew Colorado's back country better than Bridger, if you could put up with his peculiar ways. However, they could find no crossing of the formidable Continental Divide in Colorado. All that they examined were too high and too precipitously steep-sided for a railroad to negotiate. During their quest, Berthoud and Bridger located and named Berthoud Pass. Despite its 11,315 foot-high summit they recommended it to Loveland as the lowest one they could find. Upon examination, Loveland wisely rejected it for his dream railroad. For the record, no train line ever crossed Berthoud Pass. In later years, it became the first toll-free wagon road over the Continental Divide.

At a later time and in different locations there were railroads that breached the Colorado Divide. In 1904, the Moffat Railroad conquered 11,680 foot-high Rollins Pass, only a short distance northwest of Central City. A small community called Corona Station existed briefly inside an extensive snowshed on the summit. Accidents and difficulties with winter snowfall finally dictated abandonment in favor of a 6.2 mile long bore beneath James Peak. Construction

Collection of Evelyn and Robert L. Brown

North of Central City, Rollins Pass crossed the Continental
Divide. Persons who cross this pass now insist that it has
seen no maintenance since this picture was taken.

of the tunnel had long been advocated, but Southern
Colorado legislators defeated it. Then came the
Arkansas River flood of 1921. To get the Northern leg-
islators to help finance curbing the Arkansas, the
Southern legislators conceded and voted for the tun-
nel. In 1927, the Moffat Tunnel was completed.

Fremont Pass was also discovered by a surviving
mountain man, Kit Carson, who named it for explorer John C. Fremont. Two railroads crossed Fremont
Pass: the Denver, South Park, and Pacific; and the
Denver and Rio Grande. Eleven thousand, three hundred and eighteen foot high Fremont Pass is on the
Continental Divide, near Leadville, but it was too far

Collection of Evelyn and Robert L. Brown

Although this picture was labeled as Rollins Pass, its actual location is on the ridge above the ghost town of Apex. Andrew Rogers Pass crossed the Continental Divide north of James Peak.

Collection of Evelyn and Robert L. Brown

From the same vantage point, James Peak is at far left. Note the same vertical snow formation at right of James Peak and the two trails on the hillside in the middle distance.

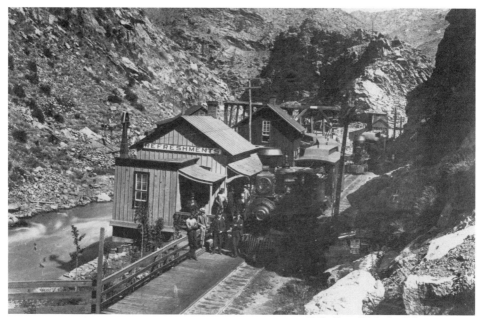

Collection of Malcolm Collier

Where North and South Clear Creek converged, photographer Joseph Collier exposed this fine picture of the small railroad settlement known as Forks Creek.

Collection of Evelyn and Robert L. Brown

Today, the highway to Idaho Springs branches to the left at Forks Creek, while the road to the right goes to Black Hawk and Central City.

away for Loveland's use. The Rio Grande Railroad also built over the Continental Divide at 10,846 foot Marshall Pass. They too used a narrow gauge to get the tracks across to Gunnison.

By the 1870s, Henry M. Teller, a Central City attorney, had assumed the Presidency of the Colorado Central. W.A.H. Loveland was the vice president until he was replaced by Oliver Ames of the Union Pacific. In August of 1871, Gilpin County's voters approved the issuance of $300,000 in county bonds for building the railroad to Black Hawk by May 1, 1872, and into Central City by June 1, an impossible time limitation. They didn't make it.

The grade up Clear Creek had to be gouged from a mountain wall and sometimes it was built over rocks piled in the creek itself. By September, there were 150 men blasting and grading in the canyon. Lieutenant Fred Grant, son of President U.S. Grant, was a superintendent until he took a leave of absence and went to Europe.

By September, work crews had passed through the Roscoe Placer Mine. After deciding that removing a huge boulder beside the placer would be more trouble than it was worth, they simply graded around it. The boulder is there even yet, making the empty site of Roscoe easy to identify. Forks Creek was their next goal. Here the North and South forks of Clear Creek come together. Later an important station would be constructed here. Forks Creek had a water tower, restaurant, and a hotel. Upon reaching the Forks, a grand excursion came up from Golden to celebrate the accomplishment. On the way up the tiny locomotive Phil Sheridan jumped the tracks twice. An excited crew and several husky male passengers lifted it back onto the rails. A reporter from the *Rocky Mountain News* made the excursion trip to Forks

Collection of Evelyn and Robert L. Brown

In this view of the Roscoe Placer the train is heading down grade toward Golden. Notice the huge boulder at the right.

Collection of Evelyn and Robert L. Brown

While constructing the Clear Creek Highway, removing the big boulder seemed too difficult. The rock still marks the empty site of Roscoe.

Collection of Evelyn and Robert L. Brown

Where the North and South Forks of Clear Creek converge, a community called Forks Creek grew up. Note the telegraph office at the left. Beyond it, the bridge carried the railroad tracks toward Idaho Springs and Georgetown.

Collection of Frances and Richard Ronzio

In this earlier view of Forks Creek a Colorado Central train is visible on the bridge at the left.

Creek and wrote that it took two and a half hours to reach the end of the tracks. His dispatch described the steep grades, 200 feet to the mile in some places. Curves and reverse curves, he wrote, were both common.

One other account noted that the grade followed the Vasquez River. At an earlier time, Clear Creek was known as the Vasquez Fork, honoring Louis Vasquez, another veteran of the mountain man era. Fort Vasquez and the obscure Vasquez Pass also bear his name. At another time, Clear Creek was called Tough Cuss Creek. Snow and frequent blizzards slowed the work in December and January. From Forks Creek the right-of-way followed the banks of the North Fork of Clear Creek. Another reporter for the *Rocky Mountain News* noted that there were twenty-five curves between the Forks and Black Hawk. He observed further, "It must have been the ambition of the original locators to make this the crookedest railroad in the world."

In January of 1872, the Grand Duke Alexis of Russia was driven up the grade on a sightseeing tour by carriage. They had gone only four miles above Golden when the cold winds forced them to retreat. When the weather cleared, construction and grading continued toward Black Hawk with an expanded work crew of 500 men. On December 11, 1872, the first work train reached Black Hawk, two full weeks ahead of a more realistic revised schedule.

According to the *Rocky Mountain News*, the tracks were laid to the old quartz mill of the New York Mining and Milling Company. This empty structure became the town's first depot. It stood at the lower end of Black Hawk. Five years later, in 1878, a more adequate stone depot was built at the opposite end of the town, replacing the mill, which was now in the

Collection of Nancy and Ed Bathke

Charles Weitfle took this picture of Horseshoe Curve, on the
grade of the Colorado Central Railroad.

way. Since the canyon is narrow here, and because
there was no way around the mill, Loveland had his
workers knock a big hole in each end of the old struc-

Collection of Evelyn and Robert L. Brown

Beaver Brook Station was on Clear Creek, northwest and behind Tunnels 2 and 3. The big pavilion was for picnics.

ture so that his trains could run directly through it to the new depot.

The financial panic of 1877 temporarily halted the final construction of a line up to Central City. Otherwise, it might have been ready for the second visit of Ulysses S. Grant in 1873. Work on that last few miles was not resumed until July 1, 1877.

General Grant loved Colorado and was here on at least five occasions. Twice his itinerary included stops in Central City. When he came in July of 1868 he was still a candidate for the presidency. He and his com-

The Yankee Hill Stage and Mail Route

JOHN WEST - - Proprietor

Makes the Trip from Yankee to Idaho Springs Every Day EXCEPT SUNDAY

Light Freight and Passengers Carried

Brinkerhoff & Preston
PROPRIETORS

The Golden Lily Mill

Yankee, Colorado
CUSTOM WORK ESPECIALLY

ALSO PROPRIETORS OF

Stage Line
Yankee to Central City

EVERY DAY EXCEPT SUNDAY

Collection of Freda and Francis B. Rizzari

These undated but very early advertisements are for the stagecoach service between Yankee Hill and Central City.

panions rode up on the stagecoach and arrived during a rain. Generals Sherman, Sheridan, and Dent were in the party, as well as Grant's son, U.S. Grant, Jr. Following a dinner in Central City, Grant's entourage boarded their coach once more and departed across Yankee Hill bound for Georgetown, where they spent the night.

Grant had already been elected to serve as our eighteenth chief executive when he returned for the second time in 1873. Grant's wife and their daughter, seventeen-year-old Miss Nellie, were members of the official party. Both Jerome Chaffee and Henry M. Teller, future U.S. Senators, journeyed down to Denver to ride with the Grants on the train and to "be seen" arriving with the Presidential group: a ploy used by members of Congress to this day.

Their special Colorado Central train left Denver's depot at 8:00 AM, following a very early parade through the city's streets. Just a short way out of Golden, their locomotive gave up the ghost, yielding to the strain of pulling a heavily loaded baggage coach up the steep grades, along with a passenger car packed with politicians. A second engine had to be dispatched, causing a delay in their arrival time at Black Hawk, and a very "antsy" mayor with his reception committee.

Since the track did not extend the remaining distance up to Central City, Grant's party left the train and rode up Gregory Gulch in horse-drawn carriages, arriving shortly after noon. All along the way spectators lined the route and waved white handkerchiefs to the dignitaries. Mrs. U.S. Grant (cross-eyed Julie), always an astute observer, asked many questions along the way and jotted down notes in a diary (which, unfortunately has not survived).

Collection of Nancy and Ed Bathke

This Joseph Collier picture looks eastward across Central City and shows a close-up view of a Colorado Central locomotive.

At the Teller House, Mayor Mullen greeted the Grants and their traveling troupe. Silver bricks, worth $13,000, from Boulder County's Caribou Mine formed a twenty-foot-long walkway from the Grant's carriage to the steps of the Teller House Hotel. What a pity that the ingots were of silver, and not gold from Gilpin

Collection of Evelyn and Robert L. Brown

In this picture of Black Hawk the town's flag pole and the Colorado Central's trestle over Gregory Street are conspicuous.

County's mines. All this happened in the midst of one of Colorado's greatest gold camps. The President was not a wealthy man and such an opulent display dazzled him

That evening a grand banquet was proffered, with Gilpin County dignitaries in attendance. The Grants dined in the adjoining Ladies' Ordinary, in clear view of those in attendance. A plush reception followed the banquet. (An ordinary was a place where meals were served at a fixed price.)

Efforts to choose a viable right-of-way for the Colorado Central to use between Black Hawk and Central City had started back in May of 1877. In the

Collection of Nancy and Ed Bathke

"Running Gulch on Wonder Rail Road" was the picturesque title assigned to this view, from half of a stereo pair by Charles Weitfle.

years since the line had reached the lower town, many new homes and commercial buildings had been finished, and some of them were in the way. The route that was finally chosen crossed Black Hawk's business district on a trestle over Gregory and Selak Streets, then continued back down the canyon to the

Collection of Fred and Jo Mazzulla

This trestle at Mountain City enabled Colorado Central and
Colorado and Southern trains to cross Packard Gulch.

south before making a switchback northward, but
higher on the hill to gain elevation prior to entering
Gregory Gulch. Using the gulch, there is a difference
of 454 feet in the mile and a quarter between Black
Hawk and Central City. The altitude at the lower town
is 8,042 feet above sea level while Central City's elevation is 8,496 feet. This disparity made it necessary
to build just under four miles of track in order to
maintain a usable grade between the two towns.
Switchbacks would be used to gain the needed elevation. Two switchbacks with bridges and trestles were
constructed. One trestle crossed Running Gulch

while the second traversed Packard Gulch at Mountain City.

In the interest of time, grading crews worked downhill from Central City as well as uphill from Black Hawk, where a massive metal bridge crossed lower Gregory Street, connecting Bates and Bobtail Hills. The late Mae Bertagnoli, who taught school in the district for many years, used to tell a story about that bridge. Trains loaded with ore and supplies crossed over the bridge at regular and frequent intervals around the clock. Whenever they crossed over the bridge a loud blast from the whistle would be heard all across the town, day or night. Mrs. Bertagnoli insisted that the sounding of the whistle at night awakened many Black Hawk residents and had a pronounced effect on the town's birthrate.

By the middle of May the construction work was finally finished. A first train steamed into Central City on May 20, although one source insists that the first traffic over the completed road arrived in Central City on May 31, 1878. It had cost the Colorado Central approximately $25,000 per mile to lay the ties and rails between the two towns, or about $100,000 for the four mile stretch.

As one might expect, a grand ball was tendered on the twenty-first. It was a gala affair, a huge celebration heralding the arrival of that first train. Hard rock miners set off noisy charges of explosives at unpredictable intervals during the day and far into the night. Six brass bands played while whistles on every mill, or on any other enterprise that had them, shrilled almost without let-up. There were longwinded political orations delivered in stentorian tones in front of the Opera House. Delegations of dignitaries from several nearby towns took part in a colorful parade.

Collection of Nancy and Ed Bathke

Charles Weitfle titled this picture "Mountain City Bridge."

Special trains brought excursionists from Georgetown, Boulder, and from as far away as Cheyenne. There was a fireman's tournament, hose cart races, and a fancy ball in the evening. All of the hotels and boarding houses were filled to capacity. The Teller House alone somehow accommodated 900 guests. One estimate placed more than 10,000 outsiders who came up for the festivities.

Collection of Fred and Jo Mazzulla

This derailment of a Colorado and Southern train occurred on a downhill run toward Black Hawk on November 30, 1919. The location was near Packard Gulch and Mountain City.

When all of the shouting was finished, the Colorado Central was still there, carrying passengers, freight, hay, grain, and mining implements on the runs uphill. On the return trips the cars were loaded with ores for the smelters. Passengers were admonished not to shoot mountain sheep from the train's windows.

The Colorado Central and some other railroads were taken over by the Union Pacific on January 1, 1881. The Union Pacific went into bankruptcy in 1893. Then came the Denver, Leadville and Gunnison, and the Union Pacific, Denver and Gulf. The Union Pacific continued to operate in Nebraska and Wyoming. A second bankruptcy occurred in

GOVERNOR
ROOSEVELT

**Republican
Candidate for
Vice-
President**

► **WILL DELIVER AN ADDRESS**
—— IN ——

DENVER

**TUESDAY.....
EVENING**

Sept. 25th

For Which Occasion The

Colorado & Southern

**Has made Extremely Low
Rates. They are:**

STATIONS	ROUND TRIP RATE	STATIONS	ROUND TRIP RATE
Greeley	$2.50	Silver Plume	32.00
Windsor	2.50	Georgetown	1.75
Fort Collins	2.00	Empire	1.75
Loveland	1.75	Lawson	1.50
Berthoud	1.50	Dumont	1.50
Longmont	1.25	Idaho Springs	1.25
Boulder	1.00	Central City	1.50
Marshall	.90	Black Hawk	1.25
Lafayette	.90		

Collection of Evelyn and Robert L. Brown

In 1900, Theodore Roosevelt visited Colorado while campaigning for the Vice Presidency on the ticket with William McKinley. These posters were used to drum up enthusiasm for the McKinley–Roosevelt ticket proposed at the 1900 convention.

Collection of Fred and Jo Mazzulla

Three of the two-foot gauge locomotives of the Gilpin Tram are
pictured in the yard at Black Hawk.

1898. At that time the Colorado and Southern was
reorganized to take over operations of its predecessor
lines. It continued to haul passengers, tourists and
freight until the line was abandoned in 1939. In 1941
the last ties were removed.

Central City's original depot is currently buried
under the huge Chain-O-Mines tailings dump. In
1968 a tourist railroad was started. After some recon-
struction, operations began and visitors were able to
ride over the old roadbed down as far as Mountain
City and return. Unfortunately, its operations were
suspended in 1980.

Down in Black Hawk there was a second railroad,
a tiny two foot gauge ultra–miniature line called the

Collection of Freda and Francis Rizzari

In Russell Gulch, a Gilpin Tram locomotive is pushing at least four loaded ore cars. The school is the brick structure on the upper street.

Gilpin County Tramway. On July 31, 1886, Andrew Rogers and his associates incorporated this unique railroad. Andrew Rogers is one of those enigmatic figures who keeps popping in and out of Gilpin County's history. He once tried to convince anyone who would listen that a tunnel under the Continental Divide was an idea whose time had come. It would provide an all weather way to connect Colorado's eastern and western slope communities. People in Central City decided that he had "static in the attic" and a few actually shunned him. Undaunted, Rogers examined an early Ute Indian trail over the Divide and constructed a wagon road over its right-of-way. It topped the range north of James Peak at 11,925 feet above sea level. It was used until better crossings were found. Today it is a long but very scenic hiking path.

But Rogers' Gilpin Tram was a better idea. Construction was started in 1887 from the railhead in Black Hawk. In all it had twenty-six miles of track. There were fifteen switchbacks. By September, one of the switchbacks had been completed into Nevadaville. It continued in operation for thirty-one years under a variety of corporate names. Most people just called it the Gilpin Tram, or simply the tram. It was always a mining railroad from its beginning to its decline.

Initially, it was built to haul ore at more reasonable costs from the properties in Chase Gulch as well as from several other areas of Gilpin County, down to the refineries and the Black Hawk railhead. On return trips it carried coal and a variety of mining supplies. In the course of just a few miles it gained about 1600 feet of elevation. Because most Gilpin County mines were separated by long distances from the processing centers down at Black Hawk, ore wagons and mule teams had long been about the only means of carting the gold concentrates, and that was expensive. Harsh winter conditions made it worse. Prior to the coming of the tram, those wagons were the only alternative.

Gilpin County teamsters turned livid when the tram was able to reduce ore hauling charges by at least a half. Still, people connected with the wagon freighting business laughed at the tram and ridiculed its tiny size. But it was successful and it probably was responsible in part for increasing the county's mineral production.

In all probability the tram's tracks had entered Central City by the end of July. In October, a Central City dog was killed while chasing the tram's little Shay engine. For the record, the first load of ore was delivered to the Meade Mill in Black Hawk on

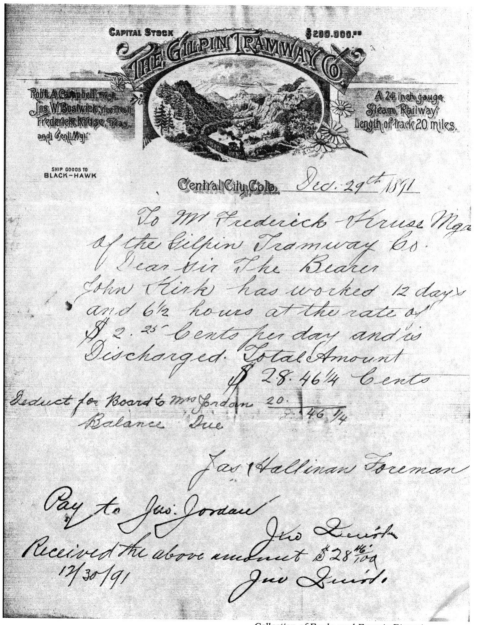

It is noteworthy in this 1891 letter that the workman in question received the princely sum of $2.25 per day.

December 14, 1887. Since their business was booming, a second Shay locomotive was delivered in 1888. It was to be used on a newly constructed branch line into Russell Gulch. Quite appropriately, the new engine was christened the Russell. A third Shay engine was delivered to Black Hawk the following year, and the teamsters quit laughing.

A severe winter struck hard at the tram in February of 1899. For a time, the little engines were unable to master the deep drifts. Service was resumed in March. Another big snow shut the Gilpin Tram down in 1913. It curtailed deliveries for several days. Incidentally, the teamsters were also unable to cope with the huge drifts. By 1890, the tram's total costs amounted to a mere $225,000.

In the present century, tourism caught on in a big way, and the public was intrigued with the possibility of riding a miniature train through the scenic back country of Gilpin County. Excursions on the tram suddenly became very popular. When the 1908 Democratic convention was held in Denver's newly finished city auditorium, 650 of the delegates rode the Colorado Central up to Black Hawk on July 11. There they transferred to ride the tram for an exciting tour before returning home. Ore cars were hastily cleaned and wooden benches were installed. Red, white, and blue bunting adorned the cars' side panels. At noon they stopped at a pretty place for a picnic, several windbag speeches, and some socializing. Miners along the way got into the act and set off many big explosions. A chorus of whistles were blown whenever they passed one of the mines. It was a gala day. They pulled back into Black Hawk at 6:00 PM. Central City's Chamber of Commerce picked up the whole tab.

1908 was the year that the Democrats nominated their most consistent loser for the third and final

William Jennings Bryan was a great advocate of free silver. He ran for the Presidency in 1896, 1900 and 1908. He lost each time. this scarce campaign button shows a clock behind Bryan, Registering 16 to 1, the ratio between gold and silver favored by Bryan.

time. Nebraska's William Jennings Bryan was a superb orator. Sometimes his detractors referred to him as the "Barefoot Boy Orator of the Platte." His dramatic Cross of Gold speech is even now a favorite at public speaking contests. Republicans nominated Taft, and Bryan lost again. He carried only three states: Nebraska, Colorado, and Nevada.

Sightseeing and aspen peeping each autumn seemed to be an idea whose time had come. Why haul only ores and merchandise, they reasoned. Why not tourists? Senator Henry M. Teller may have had a hand in starting the touring mania when he personally led an excursion on the tram on July 30, 1888. Soon the Gilpin Tram purchased a roofed excursion car for the use of touring groups. It also saw much use by tramway brass and their hangers-on

When the Gilpin Tramway's charter expired in July of 1906, it became the Gilpin Railroad. The Gilpin Railroad was a wholly owned subsidiary of the Colorado and Southern Railroad Company. This later firm operated the tram until all service was discontinued in 1917.

10.

CENTRAL CITY LANDMARKS

COLORADO WAS THE THIRTY-EIGHTH STATE to join the Union. It was admitted on August 1, 1876, just 100 years after the signing of the Declaration of Independence—hence the nickname of The Centennial State. Gilpin County led all other Colorado counties in gold production, from its beginning in 1859 until 1891–92, when gold was discovered at Cripple Creek. Within such an environment a number of important institutions and useful landmarks appeared: some of the best are still there to see and enjoy.

Until the off-year election of 1990, when Coloradans went to the polls and voted to permit limited gambling in Central City, Black Hawk, and Cripple Creek, most people thought of Central City in connection with its picturesque Opera House. This unique landmark opened its doors for the first time in March of 1878—less than two years after President Ulysses S. Grant signed Colorado's statehood bill. Just a year earlier, the Gilpin County Opera Association was created to oversee the building of an Opera House.

This Dolley photograph looks north across the Colorado and Southern depot, now buried beneath the tailings dump from the Glory Hole Mine. In this view the Catholic and Episcopal Churches and Central City's school are visible.

At this time in history, towns all across America called most of their local showplaces Opera Houses, even though these facilities were used regularly for everything from wrestling matches to Masonic dinners or minstrel shows. Central City's first show hall was the Montana Theatre. The fire of 1874 destroyed the theater, but the next year the much larger Belvidere Theatre replaced it. Although there was widespread dissatisfaction with the Belvidere, it sufficed until the completion of the new Opera House. Incidentally, the Belvidere is now the Armory Hall.

The Opera Association's memories of the 1874 fire were still fresh, so they planned for brick fire walls inside outer walls of Gilpin County granite. An ornate chandelier, with an even–hundred gas jets, provided

Courtesy Colorado State Historical Society Library

During its early years, Central City's Opera House was used for a variety of functions. Shown here is a Masonic dinner.

illumination. On opening night, specially chartered trains hauled several coaches filled with heavily perfumed first-nighters who came up from nearby towns for the grand opening. Because the Colorado Central was still under construction, coaches transported the people up the hill from Black Hawk.

In subsequent years, such luminaries as Lotta Crabtree, Lillian Gish, Edwin Booth, and Emma Abbott were among the notables who appeared in a variety of plays at Central City. Serious operas accounted for only a small part of the early offerings. Central City's Opera House was a far cry from being self-supporting. When mining went into a slump, money for cultural pursuits followed. There was one

OUR FOLKS

❦OR❧

The Tomboy.

—CAST OF CHARACTERS :—

Mrs. Thompson, good as gold,	Fannie O'Connor
Mrs. Sleeper, hoping against hope,	Chrissie Simmons
Becky Sleeper, The Tomboy,	Nina Roberts
Hulda Prime, full of complaints	Annie Warren
Silly York, slipshod, but willing	Essie Trezise
Capt. Thompson, a retired shipmaster,	Thos. Roberts
Harry Thompson, his son	Thos. Newlun
Capt Sleeper, a retired Californian,	Henry Grenfell
Teddy Sleeper, his son	Wm. Sennett
Hiram Small, a mill owner	Martin Roberts
Phil, Captain T's man of all work	T. J. Newlun

—SYNOPSIS OF INCIDENTS :—

Act. 1.—Hulda full of complaints. Becky and Teddy caught in their mischief. Captain Thompson makes complaint. Mrs. Thompson's angel of charity. Hulda gives charitable advice. Becky and Teddy take Hulda's advice. Mrs. Thompson, a friend in need. Mother and son. Shooting the basin. The rescue. "Oh ! mother : I've killed my mother."

Act 2—Capt. Thompson's soliloquy. Phil's interruption. The story of Casabianca. Becky makes friends with the captain. Hiram singing the tune of misfortune. Changing the tune. Hulda makes friends with Captain Thompson.

Act 3—The artist at work. Harry's determination. The story of unrequited love. Teddy becomes disgusted. Becky's victory unites father and son. Capt. Sleeper's return. Harry discloses his love. A united family. "OLD FOLKS AT HOME." Finale.

SPECIALTIES BETWEEN ACTS.

SEATS FOR SALE AT RICHARD ROWLING'S.

Admission, 25 cts.   Children, 15 cts.
Reserved Seats, 35 cents.

Collection of Freda and Francis Rizzari

This handbill is from an early Central City dramatic presentation.

N. H. GRENFELL, BANDMASTER.

Richard Grenfell.
Thomas Rowe.
James Bennetts.
Benjamin Waters.
Thomas Pope.

James Angwin.
Henry Grenfell.
Nicholas Grenfell.
Martin Williams.

And the Young People's Dramatic Association
FOR BENEFIT OF BRASS BAND.

THE FOLLOWING PROGRAM WILL BE PRESENTED

OVERTURE - - - (Linwood) by Band

Domestic Drama in Two Acts,

The Chimney Corner
THE CAST:

Patty Probity	Janie Angwin
Grace Emery	Mary Walters
Sol. Probity	Thomas Roberts
Peter Probity	Martin Roberts
John Probity	Thomas Newlun
Charles Chetty	John Chapple
Sifter	Jeff. Howell

During the play the following specialties will be given by the band: Song, "Killarney," James Angwin; Free Coinage Serenade, band; Johnny Chiny Polka, band; Village Festival Fantasia, band; Whittie's Quick Step, band; Express Gallop, band.

To conclude with the popular Farce,

THAT RASCAL PAT
THE CAST:

Laura (niece to Puffjacket and in love with Charles)	Mary Walters
Nancy (her maid, in love with Pat)	Janie Angwin
Pat McNoggerty (a handy servant)	M. Roberts
Major Puffjacket (on half pay)	T. Roberts
Charles Livingstone (poor but ambitious)	J. Howell

Seats on sale at R. J. Knuckey's. Usual price of admission.

Collection of Freda and Francis Rizzari

A double feature benefit performance is advertised in this time-worn handbill.

Collection of Freda and Francis Rizzari

The Second Annual Central City Play Festival in 1933 was publicized with this informative brochure.

proposal in 1881 to sell the building to the county for gutting and conversion to a courthouse. During lean years the Opera House was used for graduation exercises, political meetings, funerals, and finally for silent movies. In 1885, Buffalo Bill Cody starred in one of his clumsy plays at the Opera House.

Salvation came in 1932, when the old facility was spruced up for a festival. It opened with *Camille*, starring Lillian Gish. Ida Kruse McFarlane and Ann Evans were the leaders in the revival as well as with formation of the new Central City Opera House Association. The Association is still very active. Now each summer brings an Opera Season. Lead singers and members of the chorus are imported from San Francisco and elsewhere. Instrumental musicians are recruited locally. Plays and lighter operettas frequently alternate with ambitious productions of *La Traviata, Carmen* or other serious offerings.

In the early 1950s, the author was in the audience when Mae West brought her comical—and sometimes racy—production of *Diamond Lil* to Central City. Another time he enjoyed Max Morath's one-man show. The late George Gobel's easy going ways endeared him to the locals when he appeared in Central City. In another season, Frank Fay brought Mary Coyle Chase's *Harvey* to the old Opera House. The offerings at Central City tend to be quite varied.

The artists live in a series of cast houses, located just up the hill and across Eureka Street, while performing in Central City. Seating in the Opera House is most uncomfortable. The old wooden chairs are so close together that if you need to button your shirt, plan on stepping outside. Nevertheless, the performances are nearly always sell-outs. Reservations are suggested—far in advance during July and August.

Collection of Louis Carter

Hearses and uniformed pallbearers are observable in front of St. James Methodist Church. Across the street are the Opera House and Teller House.

Collection of Evelyn and Robert L. Brown

Here is contemporary Eureka Street, minus the funeral procession. Notice that virtually all of the landmarks from the older picture still exist.

Collection of Nancy and Ed Bathke

Lensman Charles Weitfle had a studio in Central City from 1878 to 1885. He took this picture of the interior of St. James Methodist Church, before the installation of its pipe organ.

On the opposite side of Eureka Street from the Opera House and just a few steps up the steep hill, stands the historic St. James Methodist Church, an important Central City landmark. It was organized on July 10, 1859. Actual construction began in 1864 and continued through 1868, when Cornish stone masons completed the job. St. James is Colorado's oldest surviving Protestant church. Golden's original Baptist Church was older, but it is gone now.

Aunt Clara Brown, a former slave, was a devout Methodist who came up to Central City as a laundress. Originally from Kentucky, Mrs. Brown had a laundry in Auraria before she moved up to Gilpin County. Whereas black people were not allowed on public coaches in 1859, Clara paid a miner to take her up as his hired help. Until the completion of St. James, Methodist worshipers held most of their Sunday services in Aunt Clara's log cabin. Nearly all of the recent books on Western women include information on Clara Brown. Incidentally, she saved her money until she was able to invest $10,000 in real estate. Her investments paid off quite well.

Finally, in July of 1879, St. James was dedicated. Inside, visitors may still see and enjoy a particularly fine pipe organ. It was designed, built and installed by the Steere Company of Springfield, Massachusetts, in 1898. The original cost was $3,000. It contains 874 pipes. Howard Knoll the church custodian, told us that hand-levered bellows provided wind to the instrument. Later, a water motor provided air for the same bellows. An electric blower was installed in the 1930s.

St. James is constructed on two levels. A parish hall, museum, and rest rooms are on the lower level. Banquets are often held there, as are worship services when the weather is cold. The sanctuary and the organ are on the second floor. The church is fared back into the side of a hill so steep that a door at the left of the organ opens into East High Street, the next concourse above Eureka Street.

Collection of Freda and Francis Rizzari

This Chamberlain photograph was exposed prior to July of 1872, since the Teller House does not appear in the picture. St. James Methodist Church is at the center. The long building at the junction of Eureka and Main Streets was the Montana House, where operas were presented before Central City's Opera House was completed in 1878.

Collection of Nancy and Ed Bathke

Henry M. Teller of Central City was one of Colorado's first two
United States senators.

On Sunday mornings during the opera season
members of the cast and chorus often provide sacred
music at St. James. More than sixty clergymen have
served the church: some have been part-time or stu-
dent pastors. Our dear friend, the late historian Louis
J. Carter, was of Cornish extraction and was a life-
long associate of this parish. He maintained that

TELLER HOUSE,

W. H. BUSH. Proprietor.

Central City, - Colorado.

Opened in 1872; Is elegantly furnished; First-class in all respects, and has 150 rooms.

COLLINS'
CAKE AND TART CUTTER.

Address COLLINS & CO., P. O. Box 63, Central City. Colorado.

SUBSCRIBE FOR and ADVERTISE IN

GOLDRICK'S "OLD RELIABLE"

Rocky Mountain Herald,

DENVER, - COLORADO.

$3 a year, mailed free of postage to any address, East or West.

92

Collection of Freda and Francis Rizzari

An early Teller House advertisement shared space with an inventor's device and a newspaper's promotion.

ninety-five percent of the parishioners were Cornish. St. James' current membership numbers about 140 persons.

There are those who insist that the Teller House Hotel is the most famous of Central City's landmarks. It dates from February 3, 1870, when the attorney and later Senator Henry M. Teller offered a $60,000 down payment if things could get started on a badly needed first class hostelry. Once again, the Cornish accomplished most of the construction. A fancy ball and grand opening ceremony, held on June 27, 1872, celebrated its completion. One critic compared its boxy style to a New England shoe factory or a too-tall cavalry barracks. It is five stories high and contains 150 rooms.

William Bush, a friend of H.A.W. Tabor who is suspected of introducing Tabor to Baby Doe, opened the Teller House and managed it for six years. It is of brick and stone construction and was able to survive the disastrous fire of 1874. In common with the Opera House, the Teller House's fortunes declined when Gilpin County mining went into a slump. When the Opera House made its comeback, the fortunes and revenues at the Teller House improved as well.

One of its prime attractions for visitors is inside the bar room. The fact that President Grant and other notables once stopped here now seems incidental. The big attraction for tourists is the far-famed Face on the Barroom Floor. I once had the misfortune to lead a field trip of University students to Central City in the 1970s. A tour of the Teller House was on our itinerary. Upon entering the bar our young tour guide related a colorfully embellished tale of a half-frozen miner who stumbled inside one night and tearfully painted the likeness of his sweetheart on the floor. Her narra-

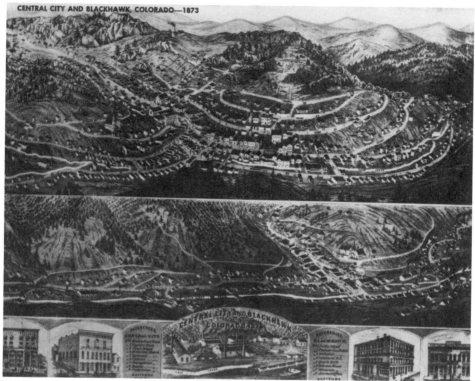

CENTRAL CITY AND BLACKHAWK, COLORADO—1873

Collection of Freda and Francis Rizzari

This somewhat idealized artist's lithograph depicts Black Hawk (misspelled as "Blackhawk") and Central City in 1873, complete with "references."

tive followed closely a well-known poem by H. Antoine D'Arcy, "The Face Upon the Floor."

The truth is far less dramatic, and this is what my students heard on the bus ride home. In 1860 the late Herndon Davis, an artist who worked for both of Denver's daily newspapers at one time or another, was commissioned to execute a series of paintings for the Teller House and the Opera House. Attorney and historian Fred Mazzulla was there one June evening when Davis got into a heated argument with Ann Evans, daughter of Colorado's second Territorial

A popular point of interest is the famous Face on the Barroom
Floor in Central City's Teller House.

Governor. Their differences revolved around the
artist's paintings of western personalities. Miss Evans
left the room in anger. One of the busboys told Davis
that he would probably be fired, a likely conclusion.
So Herndon decided to leave a remembrance.

Davis was known to have been familiar with the
D'Arcy poem. The busboy, V. Jim Librizzo, had overheard the heated exchange and felt sorry for the
artist. Librizzo also had a key to the bar. After the
Teller House had closed one night Davis purchased a
fifth of rum, a bottle of cola, and a brick with which to
roughen the floor. To avoid possible detection he is
alleged to have painted the face by candle light. It was
the face of his wife, Edna Juanita Davis, "Nita" to her
friends. Denver attorney Fred Mazzulla and Dr. Nolie
Mumey were close friends of the Davises. Both men

were sworn to secrecy, but on their respective basement floors Davis painted the faces of Mrs. Mumey and of Jo Mazzulla. The three families kept the secret of the painted face for many years, as did ex-busboy Librizzo, who worked as a bartender at Denver's Park Lane Hotel after World War II.

When Herndon Davis learned that an admission fee was being charged to view his work on the Teller House floor he was incensed. He returned to Central City, signed his name and the date on his creation. Unknown persons judiciously applied either turpentine or mineral spirits, accounts vary, and removed the signature and date, thus assuring a profitable perpetuation of the myth.

Herndon Davis passed away in 1962. Edna lived on for many years in their home at 1323 Kalamath Street. She was eighty-five years old when she died there in 1976. But the face of Edna Davis is still there, covered now with a sheet of glass and protected by a brass rail in the bar of the Teller House.

On the day after Mrs. Davis's passing both Denver papers published the real story behind The Face On The Barroom Floor in considerable detail. But somehow the more colorful legend has survived, perhaps because it is more fun.

Across Eureka Street from the Opera House and Teller House stands the law office of Henry M. Teller. It is just a small house that was built in 1862, making it one of the oldest landmarks in the city. In the interest of historic preservation the little home has been moved about several times prior to being in its present location. Although the current location is not the original one, the building itself is authentic. It survived the big fire as it was next to the Teller House in 1874 and was protected.

Courtesy Colorado State Historical Society Library

This is Senator Henry Teller's law office at its original location. That's Teller in the doorway with the derby hat.

Collection of Evelyn and Robert L. Brown

Henry Teller's law office building was moved several times. It now stands on Eureka Street, next to Williams' Stable.

Senator Teller was probably Central City's most distinguished resident. He came west from Illinois and set up his law practice in 1862. In previous chapters he has been mentioned as a one-time President of the Colorado Central, as owner of the Teller House Hotel, and in 1877 as one of Colorado's first two United State Senators. Later he was appointed Secretary of the Interior in President Chester Arthur's cabinet. This was done to create a vacancy to which Colorado's governor could appoint the unelectable H.A.W. Tabor to serve out the remaining days of Teller's term. Tabor served for an undistinguished ninety days, but was neither re-elected nor re-appointed.

Indirectly, H.A.W. Tabor's problems probably started in July of 1877 when Elizabeth and Harvey Doe arrived in Gilpin County. Harvey managed the Fourth of July Mine until it failed. When Harvey took a night job at a mill in Nevadaville, Elizabeth became the lover of Jake Sandelowski and gave birth to his child. Elizabeth was a real beauty, with a figure like a Coca Cola bottle. The miners agreed that when she walked down the street it was the best show in town. She was referred to as being "some baby." Since her name was Doe, the nickname Baby Doe soon became common. When she saw Harvey enter a brothel she filed for divorce and went to Leadville. Somehow she met H. A. W. Tabor, perhaps Bill Bush introduced them. Tabor divorced his wife, Augusta, married Elizabeth and the rest is history. Many competent Colorado History buffs insist that Tabor's marriage to Baby Doe was probably his most significant accomplishment.

Two additional women also figured in Tabor's life. Both have been overlooked by many Tabor scholars. Both were prostitutes. Willie DeVille was a Chicago

Collection of Freda and Francis Rizzari

Charles Weitfle's camera pointed north across Central City to record this view, *circa* 1875. The foreground excavation became the softball field. At lower right, a train is approaching the depot.

lady of the evening who worked at Lizzie Allen's place. She met Tabor while he was in The Windy City on a business trip. Willie became Tabor's companion and

Collection of Freda and Francis Rizzari

Taken in the winter of 1913, this picture shows the Teller House, left of center, and to its left, the Catholic and Methodist Churches. Central City's softball park and grandstand are at lower left.

traveled with him for more than a year. When Augusta discovered them they pretended to sever their affair, but still met secretly. In New York a woman learned about Tabor and Willie and attempted blackmail. Tabor told Willie that she talked too much and ended their liaison.

Prior to his marriage to Elizabeth "Baby" Doe, Tabor had a fling with Alice Morgan, a soiled dove at Leadville's Grand Central Saloon. Morgan once confided to a friend that the only way she could endure Tabor's vulgar ways and lack of cleanliness was to get drunk. During his tenure in Leadville H.A.W. Tabor owned two brothels in the city, but he never owned one in Gilpin County.

When President Arthur went out of office Teller went back to the Senate where he served until 1906. Originally a Republican, he switched parties to support William Jennings Bryan and the Democrats over the issue of Free Silver. Teller County and the ghost town of Teller City still bear his name, as do Teller School and Teller Street. Today his tiny law office may be seen, a landmark now sandwiched between the City Hall and the Williams Stable.

In most mining towns the drinking establishments were among the first to open for business, and were usually the last to close. Quite a few of them became landmarks, at least in the minds of their customers. According to State Business Directories, Central City had a total of twenty saloons in 1897, which was the peak year. There were five others down in Black Hawk. All such places were licensed and regulated by local governments. When a bond in the amount of $2,000 was paid, plus a $600 fee for a city license, a saloon could open its swinging doors. Stringent regulations stipulated that persons younger than eighteen years could not enter the premises.

In Central City all saloons were forced to close at 6 PM on Sundays and at midnight the other six days of the week. Although drinking was their principal reason for existing, most saloons encouraged card playing. Whist, Seven-Up, Poker, and Pinochle were popular. Most games and most drinking were orderly, except on Saturday nights, when more tolerance was shown by the authorities. Gang fights were uncommon, but one-on-one contests were popular and many bets changed hands on such occasions. James J. Corbett and Bob Fitzsimmons were very popular. Although they never fought in Central City, they visited there in later years. Their popularity was due to the fact that Corbett was of Irish extraction while

Collection of Frances and Richard Ronzio

In Central City, William Smitham's Saloon was a popular thirst quencher. The posters advertise Onion Lager Beer and a forthcoming circus.

Fitzsimmons was a Cornishman. Louis Carter said that $20,000 was bet in Central City on the Corbett-Fitzsimmons contest in Carson City on March 17, 1899.

Gambling with cards and dice were common while roulette wheels and Faro games were rare but not unknown. Colorado state laws prohibited gambling but they were rarely enforced unless things got out of control.

Another business that became associated with the saloons, at least in the public mind, was prostitu-

Courtesy Gilpin County Historical Society

The Henry Rothauser Saloon was in the Dostal Block on Spring Street. The bartender was August Bitzenhofer.

tion. Although the two were separated in Central City, prostitution existed nonetheless. The red light district was a small one, consisting of only two houses; and a house is not always a home. The "red light" term came from the habit of railroad men who left their lighted red lanterns hanging in front of a house or crib to indicate to others that the premises were occupied.

Black Hawk's largest and busiest brothel was located on the second floor of the Toll Gate Saloon. Central City's two parlor houses stood at the south west end of Pine Street, just a block beyond St. Mary's of the Assumption Catholic Church. After St. Mary's was built in 1892, local humorists used to say that it was possible to get saved or some other things, all on

Collection of Freda and Francis B. Rizzari

This view by an unknown photographer looks south along the
Virginia Canyon Road toward Russell Gulch. The Catholic
Church is at the far right.

the same block of Pine Street. The Coeur d' Alene
Mine and its tailings dump still stand just above the
two houses of ill fame.

Louis Carter once wrote that because they were
on a steep incline above the town, the area came to be
known as The Hill. Between three and seven ladies of
the evening engaged in prostitution in each of the two
places. Lizzie Thomas (Warwick) operated one of the
houses between 1897 and 1910. May Martin ran the
other until she sold it to Madam Lou Bunch at about
the turn of the century. Madam Lou really was a
"bunch!" She tipped the scales at more than 300
pounds for all of the years until she closed the place
in 1916.

Collection of Freda and Francis B. Rizzari

An unknown photographer took this picture of Central City from the railroad grade. The Methodist and Episcopal Churches and the school are among the many homes on the steep hillsides. James Peak is on the horizon at upper left.

In common with most of its contemporaries, Central City had the usual laws against prostitution. Also in common with other towns, such laws were generally ignored as long as public disturbances were kept to a minimum. It was widely believed that prostitution kept the worst of the men in line, making the streets safe for decent women to frequent.

In addition to the foregoing landmarks there are some other historical locations that could be of interest to the visitor. One of these is the Williams Stable, it is a brick and stone structure that was built in 1876

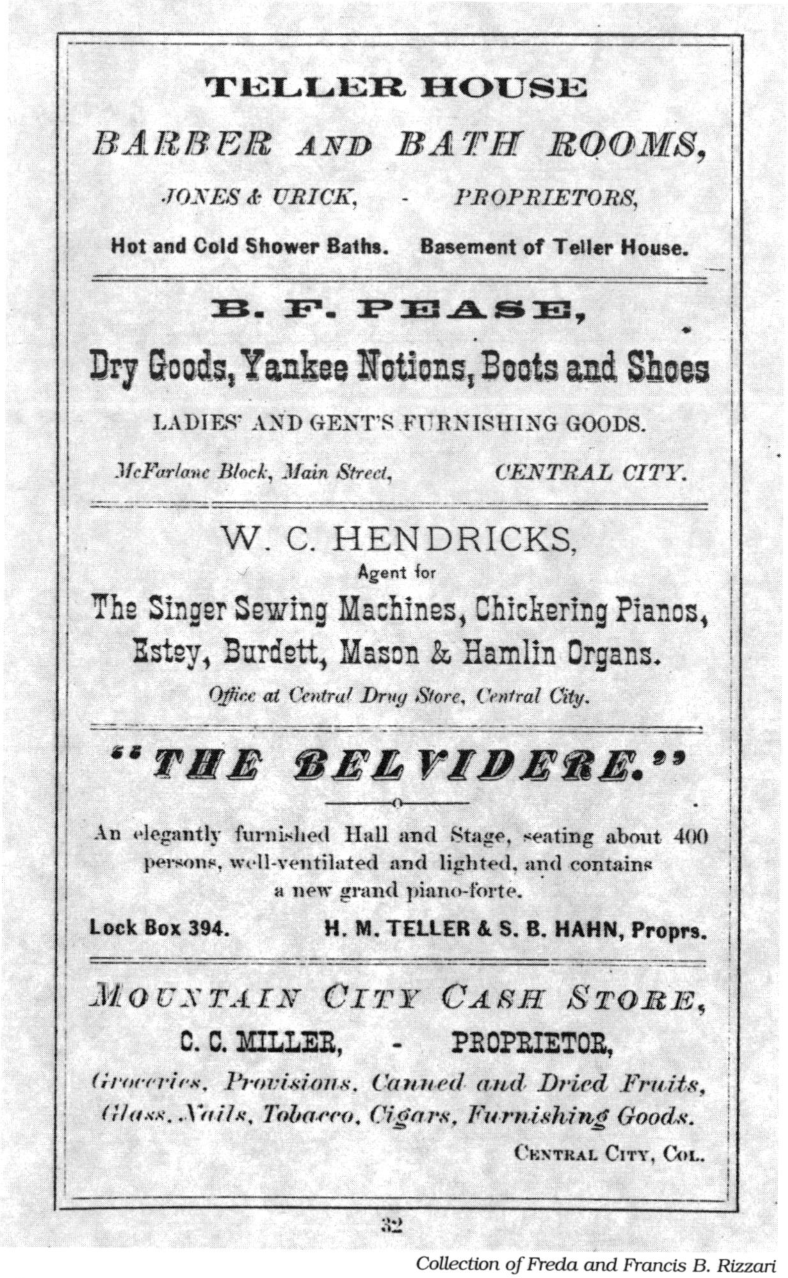

TELLER HOUSE
BARBER AND BATH ROOMS,

JONES & URICK, - PROPRIETORS,

Hot and Cold Shower Baths. Basement of Teller House.

B. F. PEASE,

Dry Goods, Yankee Notions, Boots and Shoes

LADIES' AND GENT'S FURNISHING GOODS.

McFarlane Block, Main Street, CENTRAL CITY.

W. C. HENDRICKS,
Agent for

The Singer Sewing Machines, Chickering Pianos, Estey, Burdett, Mason & Hamlin Organs.

Office at Central Drug Store, Central City.

"THE BELVIDERE."

An elegantly furnished Hall and Stage, seating about 400
persons, well-ventilated and lighted, and contains
a new grand piano-forte.

Lock Box 394. H. M. TELLER & S. B. HAHN, Proprs.

MOUNTAIN CITY CASH STORE,
C. C. MILLER, - PROPRIETOR,

*Groceries, Provisions, Canned and Dried Fruits,
Glass, Nails, Tobacco, Cigars, Furnishing Goods.*

CENTRAL CITY, COL.

32

Collection of Freda and Francis B. Rizzari

These early advertisements promote Central City establishments.

Collection of Freda and Francis B. Rizzari

Denver photographer Alex Martin took this view of Central City looking north along Main Street toward Eureka Street. The Armory, Methodist Church, and Teller House appear prominently.

as a source of fine horses and carriages for patrons of the Teller House. It is open during the Opera Season as a place where people may observe square dancing. The Ann Evans observation point is accessible from a

Collection of Freda and Francis B. Rizzari

This 1902 view shows part of the C&S Engine #9, the Methodist and Catholic Churches, and St. Aloysius Academy at upper left. Two cows seem to be standing in the snowy softball field.

point on upper Eureka Street. It provides a good view of the city below. The Pharmacy on Lawrence Street is Colorado's oldest drug store. Although it was destroyed by the 1874 fire, the owner reordered supplies and went on with the business.

Although neither St. Mary's of the Assumption nor St. Paul's Episcopal churches are as old as St. James Methodist church, both are important landmarks, housed in handsome buildings, and are well worth a visit. Central City's Armory Hall used to be the Belvidere Theatre. It was sold recently for ten million dollars and is due to become a casino. The Ida Kruse McFarlane Memorial stands on Gunnell Hill where St. Aloysius Academy boarding school stood at one time. The school was taken down in the 1930s

Collection of Freda and Francis B. Rizzari

From half of an Alex Martin stereo view we look at Central City from the east. The school and Episcopal Church are barely above center. At lower left are the tracks of the Colorado Central.

and replaced by the memorial. In common with the Ann Evans observation point, there's a nice view from here too.

The Coeur d'Alene Mine stands on Gunnell Hill, silhouetted against the sky. Each morning its whistle played "Work For The Night Is Coming." "Now the Day Is Over" was whistled in the evening. The mine was never a big producer. On First High Street, next to the Episcopal Church, stands one of Colorado's really interesting places. It was one of Colorado's first two permanent schools. Currently the building houses the Central City Museum. Finally, down at Mountain City, there is a marker of stone beside the road just below a deep vertical slash on the hillside. This is the location where John Gregory found the first lode or vein gold in Colorado. Here was the mine that started the whole Pikes Peak Gold Rush. It had to begin somewhere, and this is the place.

11.

EPILOGUE

No ACCOUNT dealing with Central City and Gilpin County would be complete without some accounting of the events, changes, and happenings that are unfolding in the current decade. State Senator Sally Hopper of Golden sponsored and eventually won support for her bill calling for limited stakes gambling in three of Colorado's mountain towns, Central City, Black Hawk, and Cripple Creek. Vigorous opposition appeared from many sources, including the governor's office. When the legislature side-stepped the issue, petitions were circulated until the needed 65,000 signatures were obtained.

On November 6, 1990, Colorado's voters went to the polls in an off-year election. Among other issues, they approved a constitutional amendment permitting limited stakes gambling in the three towns. It won approval by a healthy margin and the new law took effect on October 1, 1991.

During the most recent half century, Central City's economy has lagged badly. Concerned residents watched as the population dwindled to a scant 369 persons. Badly needed civic improvements were relegated to the back burner for lack of funds. For exam-

ple, the town's original water system was installed
sometime in the 1870s. With maintenance it has been
more or less adequate for the small year-round population. Since the approval of the gambling amendment, however, the water system seems inadequate
for increased numbers of visitors.

Prior to approval of the gaming amendment,
many local businesses had become seasonal, open
only on week-ends and during the summer "People
Season." They reasoned that small stakes gambling
could bolster tourism, bringing needed revenue into
the town's coffers and providing for a year-round
economy approaching the somewhat seasonal ski
industry in neighboring counties.

Gambling in Central City is nothing new. Prior to
1949, both wagering and slot machines appeared
annually, as if by magic, during the opera and play
seasons. The Opera Association, bars, and restau-
rants profited. To circumvent restrictive laws, the city
would assess a fine of twelve dollars each month per
machine, then levy a "John Doe" fine each autumn,
just for the record. Four gambling locations (one was
in the American Legion Hall) ran openly for bets up to
$2,000 in the summer season. An assortment of civic
improvements were paid for in this manner, until
Justice of the Peace Lowell Griffith issued warrants.
After a few arrests, the slot machines vanished.

With approval of the gambling amendment, commercial property values in Central City and Black
Hawk soared to levels no one had expected. Tax
assessments skyrocketed, too, making it impossible
for many residents to pay the new taxes on their
homes or businesses. The *Rocky Mountain News*
asserted that Central City's real estate values had
sextupled. The Chandler House sold for 2.9 million
dollars. The nearby Golden Rose Inn increased its

staff by 1,400 percent, from four to sixty. Investment money poured in from Switzerland, Holland, Great Britain, and Turkey. The historic old Teller House was renovated for gambling. Shuttle services from Denver's airport, Wheat Ridge, Lakewood, and Golden are now in operation. Several commercial parking lots have appeared in outlying areas. A number are several miles away, necessitating shuttle bus rides into Central City or Black Hawk.

Since Casinos come and go, the number currently open in Gilpin County will undoubtedly change by the time you read this. At this time, there are twenty casinos operating in Black Hawk and fifteen up in Central City. Several of those that opened their doors in October of 1991 are gone now and replaced by others. Since space is limited by the confining nature of Gregory Gulch, new buildings are under construction on nearly every open space. I recently received a call from a longtime friend, a Central City native. The family home has been sold. Taxes are now so high that he can no longer afford living in his home town. Moreover, he said that a drive of fifteen miles is necessary to buy a loaf of bread or a tank of gasoline.

A few additional observations concerning the much anticipated opening of the renovated Glory Hole may be appropriate at this time. It happened on Sunday, March 1, 1992. Now four stories tall, it became Central City's largest casino. Inside there are 326 gambling devices. It easily surpasses the Teller House, which has only 254 machines and games. The owners have combined the original Glory Hole Tavern with its next door neighbor, the Gilded Garter, plus a third adjacent building. Its interior walls now sport costly Victorian wallpaper ($250 per roll). A staff numbering approximately 200 are attired in costumes of the Victorian era. Two bars offer live entertainment.

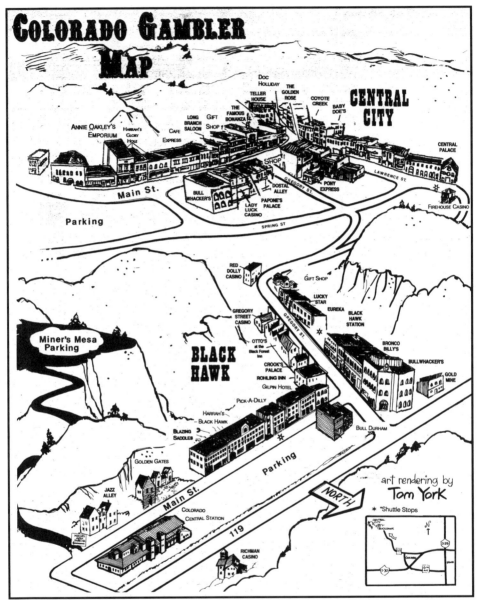

Courtesy The Colorado Gambler

Artist Tom York's rendering of Colorado casinos in 1994

The little rooms of a second floor brothel have become a series of private dining rooms. Quite apart from the bordellos located on "The Hill," mentioned in chapter ten, the second floor rooms were ancillary to the rest of the Glory Hole's functions. The Glory Hole was not merely a single purpose operation. In all, the current Glory Hole now contains an impressive 35,340 square feet of floor space.

On March 18, 1992, the *Rocky Mountain News* reported plans for a giant casino that would relegate the spacious Glory Hole to second place. Los Angeles and Las Vegas interests invested $10 million in the Gold Coin Saloon and Casino. It is already gone from Main Street. At this writing the three-story Colorado Central Station, with 600 slots, ten Blackjack and fifteen poker tables, is the largest. A lounge and restaurant occupy the third floor.

Colorado law prohibits municipal officials from holding gambling licenses, and the mayors of both Black Hawk and Central City have resigned, as have two nearby town managers—for whatever reasons.

When gamblers headed for Central City and Black Hawk on opening day, the traffic crush more than doubled on the county's winding two lane roads. Nine thousand fifty-seven cars, nearly three times the former daily average of three thousand fifty, were counted along Colorado Highway 119. Inevitably, finding parking spaces for even a fraction of this number became a problem. One Gilpin County commissioner said, "Somebody is going to have to leave the town before somebody else can come in." Other anticipated problems include regulating pawn shops, better medical services, preparing for violent crime, and regulating [?] prostitution.

Down in Golden, the State Patrol's district commander said, "Obviously, there's going to be drinking going on with gambling." When all forty-one of Central City's hotel rooms are full, people face a late night drive down Colorado Highway 119 and U.S. 6 into Golden for accommodations. Ten more troopers were requested for the city. They got five. Jefferson County decided to move its alcohol center from Lakewood to Golden. Additionally, the county hoped to convert their Administrative Services Annex Building into a detoxification center to handle the increase in drunken drivers. Community pressure from neighbors canceled both plans.

Not surprisingly, there has been a noticeable decrease in the number of students enrolled in Gilpin County schools. Why? The reason is that gambling is running families off. Corresponding increases have been noted in nearby Nederland and Idaho Springs school districts. Ever since gambling was legalized in Deadwood, South Dakota, their schools have gradually lost students, as well.

In Nederland, a short fourteen miles north of Central City, the town marshal's office has purchased two radar guns. Central City's sheriff has requested an extra $154,000 to hire three more jailers, two additional deputies, and to buy three more police cars. Sheriff Bruce Hartman hopes this will enable them to handle more drunken drivers and other offenders.

The arrival of gambling has imposed some unexpected problems as well. For instance, Gilpin County has never before needed a grand jury. Prior to 1991, the county had no need for a full-time judge. In the past, a district judge from Golden made single day visits about every three weeks. As of November 1991, Jefferson and Gilpin Counties have a joint grand jury with a full-time magistrate to handle gambling cases. Gilpin County's hundred-year-old courthouse has only one courtroom and ten jail cells.

November of 1991 brought a twenty-five percent increase in taxes, over the month of October, although slot machine income dropped by $138 per machine. An unseasonably snowy month of November may have been a factor. A total of 8.36 million dollars was generated during the initial month of gambling. Central City alone accounted for $259,653 in tax revenues while Black Hawk generated $121.353. Taxes in the amount of $495.753 went to the state for allocation between the general fund, Teller and Gilpin Counties, town governments, and Colorado's Tourism Promotion Fund.

To be better equipped in coping with unexpected problems, Central City's voters approved a new charter on December 3, 1991, making Central City a home rule city. Forty-nine persons voted for the new charter while nine opposed it. Incidentally, Central City had been one of the only three communities defined by the territorial charter, older than Colorado's constitution. Black Hawk and Georgetown now remain as the only territorial charter communities.

All things considered, what appears to be a late twentieth century gold rush has inundated Gilpin County. There were many problems that beset the original 1859 settlers and town builders, but somehow they survived and a colorful history was one of the results. Although today's problems are of a different sort and far more complex, they too will be assimilated with the passage of time. All concerned are hoping that the economic benefits of a vibrant new industry will offset any negative side effects. Central City is one of Colorado's most unique and very special places. It always has been.

BIBLIOGRAPHY

Bancroft, Caroline, *Gulch of Gold.* Denver: Sage
    Books, 1958.

Brown, Robert L., *The Great Pikes Peak Gold Rush.*
    Caldwell, ID: The Caxton Printers, Ltd., 1985.

Carter, Louis, *Yesterday Was Another Day.* Central
    City, CO: St. James Methodist Church, 1989.

Croufutt, George A., *Grip-Sack Guide of Colorado.*
    Omaha, NE: Overland Publishing Co., 1881.

Dorset, Phyllis F., *The New Eldorado.* New York: The
    Macmillan Co., 1970.

Eberhart, Perry, *Guide to the Colorado Ghost Towns
    and Mining Camps.* Chicago: Sage Books, 1972.

Griswold, Don and Jean, *Colorado's Century of Cities.*
    Denver: The authors, 1958.

Hall, Frank, *History of Colorado*, 4 vols. Chicago:
    Blakely Printing Co., 1889-1895.

Hollenback, Frank R., *Central City and Black Hawk, Then and Now.* Denver: Sage Books, 1961.

Monahan, Doris, *Destination: Denver City.* Chicago: Swallow Press, 1985.

Noel, Thomas and Leonard, Steven, *Denver, Mining Camp to Metropolis.* Niwot: University Press of Colorado, 1990.

Parkhill, Forbes, *The Wildest of the West.* Denver: Sage Books, 1957.

Perkin, Robert L., *The First Hundred Years.* Garden City: Doubleday and Company, 1959.

Smiley, Jerome C., *History of Denver.* Denver: Old Americana Publishing Co., 1978 (reprint).

Smith, Duane, *Horace Tabor, His Life and the Legend.* Boulder: Colorado Associated University Press, 1973.

Sprague, Marshall, *The Great Gates.* Boston: Little, Brown and Company, 1964.

Willison, George F., *Here They Dug the Gold.* London: Readers Union, 1952.

Williams, Albert N., *Rocky Mountain Country.* New York: Duell, Sloan and Pearce, 1950.

Wolle, Muriel S., *Stampede to Timberline.* Boulder, The author, 1954

INDEX

Opera House, 56, 162, 173-175, 178, 178, 179

Penrose, Spencer, 126
Pike, Zebulon, 2, 34
Polk, James, 33, 34
Pollock, Thomas, 51
Pony Express, 38
Purcell, James, 2, 3

Ralston, Lewis, 5
Reynolds Gang, 66
Rivera, Juan, 1
Rocky Mountain News, 36, 57, 150, 153, 206
Rogers, Andrew, 148, 167, 168
Rollins Pass, 146, 147, 148
Roosevelt, Theodore, 165
Roscoe Placer, 140, 150, 151
Russell, Green, 3-8, 14, 20, 32, 89, 92
Russell Gulch, 85-90, 91, 92, 94, 96, 126, 167, 170, 197
Russell, Majors & Waddell, 37

Saint Charles, 8
Santa Fe, 2
Santa Fe Trail, 5, 7, 19, 34
Slough, John, 62
Smoky Hill Trail, 35-37
South Park, 2
Springfield, 71
Steadman, Mike, 97, 101, 107
Steadman, Myrtle, 97,107

Tabor, H.A.W., 112, 186, 191-193

Tappan, Sam, 61
Teller, Henry, 143, 171, 184, 190, 191, 194
Teller House Hotel, 47, 53, 62, 79, 158, 159, 163, 183, 185-189, 199, 200
Toll Gate Saloon, 80, 83, 196

Utah, 1, 38

Vasquez Pass, 102, 153
Villard, Henry, 16, 18, 33, 48

West, Mae, 179
Wootton, Richens, 19, 20
Wynkoop, Ed, 7

Yankee Hill, 156
York, Mary, 23-25, 27-30, 32, 122, 123